Praise for *Lessons*

'This book lives up to its title of *Transforming safeguarding in education*, offering a practicable, whole system guide to how schools can play their part in maximising the safety and development of children.'

Eileen Munro, Emeritus Professor of Social Policy, London School of Economics and author of *The Munro Review of Child Protection*

'As a survivor of institutions that did not look after children properly, I welcome this book with real joy. Safeguarding is hard work: it means a lot of expense, devotion and time. I wonder sometimes if those on the frontline know how worthwhile their work is. Those of us who have known the damage that can be done when vulnerable people are not cared for and protected know that this is more than an important book: it is a manual for saving lives.'

Alex Renton, author of *Stiff Upper Lip: Secrets, Crimes and the Schooling of a Ruling Class*

'My former colleagues Martin Baker and Mike Glanville have used their impressive history as safeguarding professionals to write a must-read book for all practitioners with responsibility for safeguarding in education. In this increasingly complex and demanding world *Lessons Will Be Learned* focuses on the strategy of safeguarding and the importance of the effectiveness of the 'whole system'. I commend their thoughtful and well-researched approach and believe that by adopting their strategic framework, safeguarding leads in education will be better equipped to design and deliver meaningful long-term solutions for keeping children safe.'

Chief Constable Simon Bailey, National Policing Lead for Child Protection and Abuse Investigations

'As a long-standing Designated Safeguarding Lead, I am endorsing this book because it gives me hope and offers a series of solutions to the safeguarding concerns that at times overwhelm me and keep me awake at night. The chapter on The Challenges of Change is very pertinent and now. There is not a safeguarding lead in the country who is not run ragged by the current Covid-19 situation. This book acknowledges and supports the hard work done in schools to keep children safe and offers opportunities to work more effectively and smarter. An easy and very beneficial read for all those involved in safeguarding our children.'

Sue Bailey MBE, Safeguarding Lead, The Arthur Terry Learning Partnership

'I wish I had this book 10 years ago when I started working in education. The techniques and habits of mind set out in this book are a gift to anyone who has to think about safeguarding children. *Lessons Will Be Learned* is filled with insights that apply to all educators.'

Elena Benito Molina, Europe Chief Operations Officer and Spain Managing Director at Inspired Education Group

'Having read this gem of a book the advice and information really made me think about safeguarding in my own school. It excited me and made me look at safeguarding very differently, opening my eyes to meaningful strategic development and how all stakeholders can be involved in evolving the process holistically rather than it just being a legal process that we have to comply with. If you follow the guidance and support within this book you can't go wrong. I honestly think that anyone involved with the management and leadership of any school needs to read this.'

Caroline Newman, Headteacher, Gladstone Primary School, Barry, Vale of Glamorgan

'This book should be compulsory reading for all safeguarding leads as a very practical guide on how to turn compliant safeguarding policy into excellent safeguarding practice. It is particularly helpful as it explains the overarching principles of creating a positive safeguarding culture within a school and also goes into the details of how particular safeguarding issues are best handled. This is the book that will help you sleep at night as a DSL.'

**Luke Ramsden, Senior Deputy Headteacher,
St Benedict's School, Ealing, London**

'This book gives practical and sensible support for school leaders who are both experienced and new to the DSL role in a school. A 'must' purchase for all Headteachers that will help develop the important work of safeguarding children in all our schools.'

Angela Maxted, Headteacher, Cheriton Primary School, Kent

'Safeguarding often comes at a cost; not only to the vulnerable who we all have a duty to protect but also to those individuals who support them, the people who regularly go home worrying, did they get it right? Have they done enough? Too often, for want of a sensible and workable strategy, we see organisations flounder and fail, usually not through a lack of care, but because of a failure in approach. This book not only supports strategy, it also helps those individuals who may feel overwhelmed, lost, and alone.'

Jackie Shanks, Executive Headteacher

'An absolute must read for any safeguarding lead who wants to have a more strategic, proactive approach to safeguarding in their school. Whether you're new to the role or an experienced safeguarding lead this book helps you delve into your current approach, analyse it and make a clear path to creating a more proactive culture in your school!'

**Vikkey Chaffe, Founder of Primary School Leaders and
previous Primary School Senior Leader with safeguarding
responsibility**

'This book will be an invaluable read for Designated Safeguarding Leads in schools and colleges. Martin and Mike's years of experience within the police and now within and supporting education with safeguarding issues provides the reader with helpful and pragmatic advice, guidance and knowledge. Having trained Designated Safeguarding Leads for the last 15 years, this book covers all aspects of the role and addresses the concerns and worries that they may have about taking on the position. It is easy to read, engaging, and the key learning points at the end of each chapter are a great reference point.'

**Sara Rogers, Education Safeguarding Manager,
Cambridgeshire County Council**

'This book reminded me again of how complex and difficult the role of a safeguarding lead is. Importantly, every part of this book felt familiarly grounded in good sense and best practice, obviously from many years of real, lived experiences. A great companion to daily decision making and safeguarding leadership.'

**Paul Turner, Head of School Standards, Safeguarding and
Inclusion at Blackpool Council**

'This much needed practical resource for safeguarding leads talks not in academic terms but from the vast experience of its authors. These complex issues are often experienced by the schools and Trusts I advise and this book will help support all schools and trusts in developing and enhancing their standard of safeguarding.'

Dai Durbridge, Partner, Browne Jacobson LLP

'If you have anything to do with children, young people or vulnerable adults I implore you to read this book. Safeguarding is all our responsibilities, but it's hard, so very hard. *Lessons Will Be Learned* will help you understand the basic principles, right the way through to the difficult decisions you have to make. The good news is you're not alone. Help is at hand. And thank goodness for that.'

**Neil Watkins, CEO, Everything ICT (Department for
Education 'Every Child Matters' team 2003-2010)**

'I have worked in education for over 20 years and this is the first time I have come across anything that is so comprehensive about safeguarding. I would suggest that it should be *the* book of safeguarding within schools.'

Nick Finnemore, founder, director and EdTech thought leader, Finnemore Consulting

'Feeling safe makes learning possible! However, investigating the U-turns and uncertainties of the ever-changing safeguarding landscape adds an additional burden to already overstretched educators. So, this timely book is a real find – a must have! Written by experts in the field, it provides clear insights, practical tips, and advice, making the complex seem straightforward.'

Karine George, Consultant Researcher, former Headteacher and award-winning educationalist

'I'm a firm advocate for understanding the *why* in any given practice. This book provides the *why* of safeguarding in education and is quite simply, a must read. The eight combined elements outlined give a 'whole system' approach, providing a framework for achieving outstanding safeguarding. Read it, share it – and do it.'

Keith Mabbutt, Founder & CEO, The Street Soccer Foundation

'This book encapsulates a strategic, thoughtful, comprehensive and holistic, practical and academic guide to the myriad issues and responsibilities of all those concerned with safeguarding. Whether in a Governor, or trustee and director role, including senior leadership, this book is aimed at everyone involved in the wide spectrum of safeguarding issues. It's an essential guide with real life experiences shared by both authors who were former distinguished senior police officers, providing insight into every aspect of safeguarding and I commend it to you.'

Barry Harwood, Lawyer and founder of Harwood Law; Barrister member of the National Bar Council for England & Wales

'Lessons Will Be Learned will be a valuable lifeline for leaders struggling with the weight of safeguarding within their educational settings. Martin and Mike's insights and years of experience at the forefront of policing come together to provide pragmatic and supportive advice and techniques to cope with one the most challenging issues facing the education system currently, safeguarding our nation's children. The book's approachable tone and acknowledgement of the loneliness, worry and anxiety that besets many school leaders with safeguarding responsibilities will help reassure practitioners as well as providing access to easy to follow processes and safeguarding tools. Congratulations to Martin and Mike for sharing their insights and guidance on this vitally important issue.'

Caroline Wright, Director General, British Educational Suppliers Association (BESA)

'Process in safeguarding has become onerous and expensive, often without clear improvement in outcomes for those most vulnerable. This book is a key support tool for leaders in this area, enabling them to take a more strategic view, providing a robust "whole system" approach.'

Rob Whiteman CBE, CEO, CIPFA (The Chartered Institute of Public Finance and Accountancy)

'This is a significant new book that deals with safeguarding young people, a subject that has long been under-examined by academics, policymakers and practitioners. Drawing on their considerable experience not only as senior police officers but also as the founders of an award-winning technology firm set up to deliver solutions to the challenges of safeguarding, the authors provide leaders of educational establishments with a clear strategic approach to safeguarding by identifying what needs to be done to improve the management of this important discipline.'

Professor Dylan Jones-Evans OBE, Assistant Pro Vice Chancellor (Enterprise), University of South Wales

LESSONS WILL BE LEARNED

Transforming safeguarding in education

MARTIN BAKER AND MIKE GLANVILLE

First published in Great Britain by Practical Inspiration Publishing, 2021

© Martin Baker and Mike Glanville, 2021

The moral rights of the authors have been asserted

ISBN   9781788602716 (print)
        9781788602709 (epub)
        9781788602723 (mobi)

Every effort has been made to trace copyright holders and to obtain their permission for the use of copyright material. The publisher apologises for any errors or omissions and would be grateful if notified of any corrections that should be incorporated in future reprints or editions of this book.

 Practical Inspiration
Publishing

There are no words to express how grateful we are to Trudi and Sara for sticking with us on our crazy life journeys, and for giving us the time and space to write this book in our 'free time'; we just had to get it out of our heads.

~

We dedicate this book to the educators who safeguard children and young people, wherever they may be. In every sense you are truly life savers.

Contents

List of abbreviations

ACEs	Adverse Childhood Experiences
ACPCs	Area Child Protection Committees
CAMHS	Child and Adolescent Mental Health Services
CCGs	Clinical Commissioning Groups
CSPR	Child Safeguarding Practice Reviews
CYPMHS	Children and Young People's Mental Health Services
DPIA	Data Protection Impact Assessment
DPO	Data Protection Officer
DSL	Designated Safeguarding Lead
DSP	Designated Senior Person
EHCP	Education, Health and Care Plan
FGM	Female Genital Mutilation
FSM	Free School Meals
GDPR	General Data Protection Regulation

GIRFEC	Getting It Right for Every Child
ICO	Information Commissioner's Office
IICSA	Independent Inquiry into Child Sexual Abuse
IRMS	Information and Records Management Society
ISI	Independent Schools Inspectorate
KCSIE	*Keeping Children Safe in Education*
LADO	Local Authority Designated Officer
LSCB	Local Safeguarding Children Board
MASH	Multi-Agency Safeguarding Hubs
MAT	Multi-Academy Trust
SCR	Serious Case Review
SEL	Social and Emotional Learning
SEN	Special Educational Needs
SENCO	Special Educational Needs Coordinator
SEND	Special Educational Needs and/or a Disability
SMART	Specific, Measurable, Achievable, Relevant, and Time-based
SPP	Service Pupil Premium

Foreword

As a safeguarding practitioner I have been 'known to the police' for a long time (in a good way!), as founder and Director of the Cardiff Women's Safety Unit, as the Assistant Police and Crime Commissioner for South Wales Police and through delivering the setup of Independent Domestic Violence Advisors and Multi-Agency Risk Assessment Conferences from an idea to a UK service. Consequently, I have worked alongside many police officers, so when I first met Martin and Mike – still fresh out of their blue serge uniforms – my initial thought was 'what are these two ex-coppers up to?' Well, I found out when I read this book.

At last! In one place, a holistic view of safeguarding in education and a clear vision for anyone in a leadership position. The case for a robust and systematic approach to keeping children safe in nurseries, schools and colleges has been well made by countless case reviews of child deaths and those involving serious harm. Children spend nearly a third of their lives in school and this book is a toolkit for making that experience so much safer, enhancing their wellbeing and promoting their sense of self.

Schools and colleges are, for many children and young people, the place in which they feel safe and a place to make and meet friends, so that they can grow as people as well as learn. School staff have always reached out to those children and young people who may be worried or even frightened, and they know when a child is hungry, tired, or needing care. All children have a right to a safe childhood; we know that adverse childhood experiences are cumulative and have a huge impact across the rest of their lives.

Now, schools and colleges are key partners in keeping children safe, working alongside police, social care and other agencies, and in some cases even becoming safeguarding hubs themselves. We train all school and college staff in safeguarding; we have a designated professional lead on safeguarding; and many schools and colleges now have electronic systems such as MyConcern managing the recording of concerns. These systems allow staff to accurately track and theme safeguarding risk and need from the low level – perhaps being hungry on one day because they missed breakfast – to the child who is always hungry, always tired as they do not have a bedtime or are scared to go to sleep. Children who we all know smell, as no one cares enough to wash their clothes or ensure that they are clean.

Neglect is an emotional harm as well as a lack of physical care; not having an interested adult in a child or young person's life says, 'you are not important, and you do not matter'. Reviews of child deaths and those involving serious harm have consistently shown us that we need to remain vigilant to these 'low level' concerns so that, over time, we have the evidence to act to protect children and young people.

As thresholds for referrals to Children's Social Care inexorably rise safeguarding falls back onto schools to meet the root cause of the problem. Even experienced safeguarding leads can struggle with the stress of managing the risks and meeting the needs of our most vulnerable children and young people. It is a tough job. In years to come I think we will look back and be amazed that most school and college staff did this without proper safeguarding supervision.

One of the many things we have learnt since the onset of Covid-19 is the critical importance of schools in keeping children and young people safe from harm. We saw in the first lockdown that when schools closed, safeguarding referrals fell dramatically and yet we knew that families were struggling. We have seen over lockdown an increase in domestic abuse, non-accidental child death, mental health issues and a massive demand being placed on foodbanks. Yet, concerns about children fell. And we now know that the number of reported incidents of children dying or being seriously harmed after suspected abuse or neglect rose by 27% after England's first 2020 lockdown.

Families were thrown together with all the pressures of working from home and living without the support from friends and extended family. Add to this for some families the pressures of cramped space, the need to provide education at home, the risk of job losses and money worries. It was then that the crucial role schools play in ensuring the wellbeing of all our children became clear to everyone. Schools are not just about learning, they ensure that children and young people are fed, cared for and kept safe.

This book is an essential guide for those involved in a leadership role in safeguarding in education. It is practical, helpful, and based on the values that underpin outstanding safeguarding practice. *Lessons Will Be Learned* can help us all as individuals or institutions to do the best we can to make a positive difference to children's lives, takes us on a journey of how we should do this and is a real tour de force on the subject of safeguarding in any educational setting.

Jan Pickles OBE

Introduction
Safeguarding in education
The leadership challenge

This book is for leaders of safeguarding in education and will help you to bring a strategic approach to the business of keeping children safe. While the principles we'll be exploring apply to pretty much any sector, we're focusing on education because it's an area we know extremely well and one in which we can envisage a significant impact from a new approach.

We've been directly involved with safeguarding for much of our professional lives, starting with our roles as senior police officers (one of us as a Chief Constable and the other as an Assistant Chief Constable). During our police service we each had personal responsibility for child and adult safeguarding in a variety of contexts, and we each have roles in education governance today. This has given us both a passion and commitment to the transformation of safeguarding in schools and colleges, and to support all staff, particularly safeguarding leads, to succeed in their roles.

We know that being a safeguarding lead is a huge responsibility.[1] You have a duty of care not only towards the children for whom

---

[1] Safeguarding leads in education have different job titles across the UK. In England, they're 'Designated Safeguarding Leads' (DSLs); in Wales,

you're responsible but also to the parents and caregivers who've put their trust in you. This was illustrated at one of our 2019 safeguarding conferences, attended by representatives from 140 schools, at which we were privileged to have Alex Renton talk about his own experience as a victim of abuse at school. Alex is an award-winning journalist and author whose book, *Stiff Upper Lip*,[2] recounts his and others' experience of abuse in British boarding schools; he also made an ITN documentary that featured testimonies from many victims. At our conference, Alex had only just launched into his presentation when he had to step back to compose himself. It was probably only for a few seconds, but it felt like longer. Eventually he said, 'I'm sorry, I just can't believe that all you people are here, focused on preventing the sort of thing that happened to me and the other people who suffered. I just could not be more grateful and impressed that you're dedicated to doing this.' It was one of the most humbling experiences of our professional lives.

It's so easy to forget what good safeguarding (what Alex Renton describes as 'the real job of properly caring for the vulnerable') means. It can make the difference between long-term misery and happiness, harm and safety, even life and death. For a safeguarding lead this can be pretty scary. You have a duty to protect the children you're responsible for, and if you fail in that the consequences can be huge and life-long.

Not only do you have this responsibility, but it's hard work. We live in an increasingly complex world that doesn't always have children's best interests at heart, and sometimes even sets out to harm them. You couldn't be doing a more important job, and yet it's unlikely that you have all the support you need. You might go

---

'Designated Senior Persons' (DSPs); in Northern Ireland, 'Designated Teacher for Child Protection'; and in Scotland, 'Designated Child Protection Officers'.

[2] A. Renton, *Stiff Upper Lip: Secrets, Crimes and the Schooling of a Ruling Class*. W&N, 2018.

home wondering if you've missed something crucial, or worrying about someone you aren't sure how to help.

This nagging doubt is probably down to you being so busy firefighting, or dipping in and out of your work, that you're rarely able to stand back and see the bigger picture. Safeguarding is something you *do* rather than think deeply about. And if you work in education, particularly in a primary school, it's likely that the job of being the safeguarding lead came as one of your many responsibilities in another demanding senior role; many safeguarding leads are 'anointed' with or inherit the role in this way. Alternatively, you may have volunteered for it, seeing it as an essential part of your professional development – one in which you believe you can make a difference.

Irrespective of how you came to safeguarding, this is the book that will help to transform your practice, by providing you with a comprehensive strategic framework and practical advice on how to transform your safeguarding. We'll walk you through the eight principles of a structured approach that will enable you to spot problems before they arise, deal with them more effectively when they do, and build a network of support both within and outside your organisation. Throughout, we'll give you examples and stories that highlight the various aspects of our unique approach. As we mentioned before, they're mainly relevant to education, but there are other settings to which they also relate. Whatever the organisation you work in, safeguarding leads like you all have one thing in common – a requirement to protect children to the very best of your ability.

Safeguarding today

But first, how did safeguarding come to be the undertaking that it is now? Abuse, harm and neglect are nothing new, but as time has gone by our society has changed dramatically in terms of the behaviour it considers to be legally and morally acceptable.

Indeed, in the past certain acts that we now consider to be child abuse were seen as anything but. However, while there have been momentous changes in both our legal and moral codes, human nature and history both lead us to the conclusion that dangers to children will never be eradicated; in some cases those dangers have even been increased by developments such as social media. This is no more clearly stated than in the words of Leonard Pozner, whose six-year-old son Noah was murdered in a mass school shooting at Sandy Hook Elementary School in Connecticut:

> We weren't prepared for the internet. We thought the internet would bring all these wonderful things, such as research, medicine, science, an accelerated society of good. But all we did was hold up a mirror to society and we saw how angry, sick and hateful humans can be.[3]

Since the 1970s, child protection legislation, policy and procedure have gone through fundamental changes; we can see this from the plethora of government guidance and recommendations that have resulted from multiple case reviews.[4] While this has gone some way towards preventing and reducing harm, there's clear evidence that safeguarding concerns are still significant issues throughout our society and across all age groups.[5] What's more, a substantial proportion remains unreported.

---

[3] H. Freeman, 'Sandy Hook father Leonard Pozner on death threats: "I never imagined I'd have to fight for my child's legacy"', *The Guardian*, 2 May 2017. Available from www.theguardian.com/us-news/2017/may/02/sandy-hook-school-hoax-massacre-conspiracists-victim-father [accessed 17 December 2020].

[4] Each UK nation has its own statutory or other governmental guidance for safeguarding in education: *Keeping Children Safe in Education* – KCSIE (England); *Keeping Learners Safe* (Wales); *Safeguarding and Child Protection in Schools* (Northern Ireland) and *The National Guidance for Child Protection in Scotland*. See Appendix A for full details.

[5] 'Adult safeguarding was described to us as the "poor relation" of safeguarding arrangements, with inconsistent local partnership work to consider what protections or support might need to be put in place for

To give you some idea of the scale of child safeguarding issues in England today, in 2019–20:

o 642,980 children were referred by public agencies to local authority children's social care departments because of concerns about their welfare;

o 389,260 children were legally defined as being a 'child in need';

o 51,510 children were subject to a formal child protection plan;

o 18.2% of all referrals to social care were made by schools (117,010); and

o 56% of children in need had abuse or neglect as their primary need identified at assessment.[6]

Ongoing developments in the safeguarding policy framework and increased awareness and training across the public sector may have been partial causes for these high numbers. Even taking that into account, it's not just the scale of the problem that's increased. The range of safeguarding concerns has exploded to include new issues such as child sexual exploitation, child criminal exploitation (including 'County Lines'), female genital mutilation (FGM), grooming, online safety, peer-on-peer abuse, radicalisation, sexual violence, and upskirting, many of which have triggered new legislation. In addition, there's been a significant increase in the number of young people with mental health issues, with self-harm being a common problem.

---

vulnerable adults.' HM Inspectorate of Constabulary and Fire & Rescue Services (HMICFRS) and HM Crown Prosecution Service Inspectorate (HMCPSI): July 2019. Available from www.justiceinspectorates.gov.uk/ hmicfrs/wp-content/uploads/crimes-against-older-people.pdf [accessed 1 January 2021].

[6] Department for Education, 'Characteristics of children in need: 2019 to 2020'. Available from https://explore-education-statistics.service.gov.uk/ find-statistics/characteristics-of-children-in-need/2020 [accessed 5 January 2021].

There is also research-based evidence from around the world clearly showing that potentially traumatic events that occur in childhood (from birth to age 17) – known as ACEs, or Adverse Childhood Experiences – can have a significant and life-long impact on a child's health and wellbeing. ACEs include many types of abuse, harm and neglect and often involve domestic violence, parental mental illness, and drug and/or alcohol abuse.[7, 8]

The research conducted in the United States by the Centers for Disease Control and Prevention – the CDC-Kaiser Permanente Adverse Childhood Experiences (ACE) Study – was one of the largest-ever investigations of childhood abuse and neglect and household challenges and later-life health and wellbeing.

The ACEs that were identified included experiencing violence, abuse or neglect; witnessing violence in the home; having a family member attempt or die by suicide. Other notable risk factors included those aspects of a child's environment that can undermine their sense of safety, stability and bonding, such as growing up in a household with substance misuse; mental health problems; or instability due to parental separation or incarceration of a parent, sibling or other member of the household.

---

[7] For more information, see www.cdc.gov/violenceprevention/aces/index.html www.cdc.gov/violenceprevention/pdf/preventingACES.pdf

[8] In children's social work and in some other professions these three issues – domestic violence, parental mental illness, and drug and/or alcohol abuse – have become known as 'the toxic trio', because of a suggested cumulative effect that significantly multiplies the risk to children when they occur together. However, recent research led by the National Children's Bureau and the Universities of Cambridge and Kent has cast doubt on this hypothesis, stating that '...there is very little understanding of how, and indeed if, they combine to significantly increase the danger to children'. Parents have also felt stigmatised by the use of this term. National Children's Bureau, 'Poor evidence around "toxic trio" poses questions for child protection', 23 November 2020. Available from www.ncb.org.uk/about-us/media-centre/news-opinion/poor-evidence-around-toxic-trio-poses-questions-child-protection [accessed 29 November 2020].

Research in Wales has found that people who report experiencing four or more ACEs are, as adults:

o three times more likely to suffer from heart disease, respiratory disease or type 2 diabetes;
o four times more likely to be a high-risk drinker;
o six times more likely to never or rarely feel optimistic;
o 14 times more likely to have been a victim of violence in the last 12 months;
o 15 times more likely to commit violence;
o 16 times more likely to use crack cocaine or heroin; and
o 20 times more likely to go to prison.[9]

And what happens to adults with six or more ACEs, as opposed to four? They can die 20 years earlier than those who have none, and are 14 times more likely to attempt suicide. Furthermore, ACEs can be a family legacy that is passed from one generation to another; when people who have experienced ACEs become parents themselves, there is clear evidence that some (but by no means all) will have the potential to inflict the same awful experiences they suffered upon their own children. In the words of Dr Robert Block MD FAAP, President of the American Academy of Pediatrics, 'Adverse childhood experiences are the single greatest unaddressed public health threat facing our nation today.'[10] In our view, the impact of ACEs alone shows the critical need for effective safeguarding in education.

Of course, safeguarding challenges aren't confined to 'ordinary' schools and colleges – children's centres, nurseries, independent schools, pupil referral units, virtual schools,[11] higher education settings,

---

[9] Public Health Wales, *Adverse Childhood Experiences and Their Impact on Health-harming Behaviours in the Welsh Adult Population*, 2015.
[10] Centers for Disease Control and Prevention, 'About the CDS-Kaiser ACE Study'. Available from www.cdc.gov/violenceprevention/childabuseandneglect/acestudy/about.html [accessed 17 December 2020].
[11] Virtual schools in England are operated by local education authorities to promote the educational achievement of looked after children (LACs)

multi-academy trusts (MATs) and English-medium international schools are also responsible for safeguarding their learners, as are their CEOs, governors, directors, trustees, and proprietors. And the safeguarding of children and young people who are home-educated, have special educational needs (SEN), are 'looked after children' or 'previously looked after children' (often referred to as LACs and PLACs), or who have serious social, emotional and mental health needs creates an additional complexity.

But that's okay, because there's additional funding to deal with all this, isn't there? Indeed, it could be argued that 'more money' has gone into education and other services such as Child and Adolescent Mental Health Services (CAMHS), but significant cuts to local authority and other public sector budgets have led to a substantial reduction in resources in key aspects of both child and adult safeguarding. And even where there has been 'more money' there has been an even larger increase in demand for services or in other costs.[12] The outcome has been that some of the workload that has traditionally been the responsibility of other agencies is now falling to your school or college. As a consequence, an increasing proportion of staff time and education resources is being spent on safeguarding, with the level of demand often outstripping the capacity of you and your staff to deal with it.

---

and previously looked after children (PLACs). They are responsible for managing Pupil Premium funding for the children they look after and for allocating it to schools and alternative provision settings – see www.gov.uk/ guidance/pupil-premium-virtual-school-heads-responsibilities. Following recent government consultation, the responsibilities of virtual schools may be extended to include children in need (CIN) and children in care (CIC).

[12] 'Our analysis suggests that, in 2017/18, 43% of CCGs had increased their CAMHS budgets by less than the extra money they had been allocated for children's mental health. In those areas, it seems that some of the extra money was in fact spent on other priorities.' YoungMinds, 'Children's mental health funding: Where is it going?' 30 October 2018. Available from https://youngminds.org.uk/blog/childrens-mental-health-funding-where-is-it-going/ [accessed 11 January 2021].

The result is a landscape of higher demand, more responsibility and more complex work, but with fewer means to manage it. You need to know more, and do more, than ever before.

Safeguarding in education – the business case

We can add to the equation 'more to deal with divided by fewer resources' the increasing pressures you're under to perform to the highest standards. From our regular conversations with school and college staff, we know that the ever-increasing scrutiny in this area raises in their minds the possibility of disciplinary action or legal sanctions if they get something wrong. Also, parents and caregivers are increasingly willing to challenge staff on how they do their jobs, which can result in formal complaints, civil litigation or other court proceedings. In the worst cases, there is the potential for criminal proceedings for misconduct in public office or civil proceedings for negligence to be brought against safeguarding practitioners who have seriously failed in their duties. More likely is some form of professional disciplinary action that could be career-ending. For proprietors, directors and trustees of MATs, or independent schools, action could also be taken under company or charity law.

Not only is this a cause for personal concern, but you have your organisation to think of as well. The quality of your safeguarding can have serious implications for your school's ability to work with other agencies to protect children, its reputation, how easy it finds it to attract and retain quality staff, its legal compliance, the gradings it achieves from its audits and inspections, and in some (albeit rare) instances its continued existence.

Safeguarding strategy

Even though the picture we've painted seems grim, we know there's also a deep satisfaction in protecting children and that you want to do it well. Amidst all of the challenges, let us not lose sight of the benefits of successful safeguarding; 'woe is me' is not what we are saying here. What we are arguing for is a focus on getting well organised to deliver the two greatest benefits of effective safeguarding – the safety of children from both immediate and life-long harm and the success of educators in developing children and helping them to fulfill their potential. In the MAT of which I am a director, one of our key values is that 'learning is everything', and that means that every child has to be safe and be given the means and opportunity to learn. And that's what successful safeguarding delivers. That's why we're focusing on the *strategy* of safeguarding in this book, rather than giving you a list of to-do points or short-term tactics. You'll find a few of those as you go along, but the main thing you'll learn is how to step back from your practice and identify what you need to improve in a systematic way – one that looks at your whole safeguarding system rather than your day-to-day activities. The increased complexity and volume of safeguarding cases, combined with the reduction in resources, means that safeguarding must move beyond firefighting and into measured, long-term thinking.

Let's take a look at the benefits of this strategic approach. It will help you to:

o   gain the internal and external support that will help you to do safeguarding well;
o   discover what information you need to prevent harm and protect children;
o   manage cases professionally;
o   work with external agencies in such a way that you each gain what you need from the other;
o   understand the true power of data and information;
o   *actually* learn the lessons from your own professional practice and that of others;

o take a team approach to safeguarding, managing and developing other staff in your school so they can support you; and

o keep your knowledge and skills fresh so you can be effective in what you do.

These elements combine to help foster a culture of safeguarding, and together they provide a 'whole system' approach. We believe that this is so fundamental to achieving effective safeguarding that we have devoted a chapter to each of the eight principles within the model. While the model can be interpreted as a cyclical clockwise process, you will see that all of the principles are inter-connected. This reflects the reality of really good safeguarding practice where these principles comes together to create a safeguarding 'safety net' for both children and practitioners.

Figure 1: A strategic approach to safeguarding

Excellent safeguarding should be a comprehensive, joined-up system based on sound principles that puts the child at the centre, not a collection of independent activities in separate silos. The approach we are advocating prompts you to consider everything that is going on in that child's 'universe', not simply the current issue in isolation.

Your establishment has a unique window on the world of the children and young people within it. In fact, people working in education have more day-to-day contact with children during their waking hours than any other agency (and, in some cases, more than their parents or carers), which means you're more likely to spot concerns at an early stage. This means you can gather information to create knowledge, which in turn leads to understanding. And then you can do something about it. That's why being strategic is so important, otherwise information is just noise.

We realise you might be thinking, 'Well, it's great to know the principles of safeguarding and how to view it strategically, but I want to know *what* to do and *how* to do it', and that is entirely valid. However, we trust that once you know the 'why' of excellent safeguarding practice it will help to put into context the 'what' and the 'how', only some of which we have included in this book. You are able to access the majority of the 'what' and the 'how' from other, more 'real-time' resources. This is important, because the 'what' changes on a regular basis as new safeguarding risks and threats arise, to say nothing of the ever-changing guidelines that permeate the sector, and the regional variations across the UK and local authority areas.

Also, you don't need us to tell you that each area of safeguarding can require radically divergent actions and tactics. For instance, taking a disclosure from a child requires a completely different skill set to creating an anti-bullying programme or talking to a parent about a student's suspected drug abuse. It would be an unwieldy book that told you how to approach every single issue, and it would also be out of date in no time. Given that there's plenty of operational advice already available on the 'how to' elements of safeguarding, we don't propose to replicate it here. What we're seeking to provide is a transformational approach that will support you to be a proactive and visionary leader of safeguarding.

The paper trail

When we first started working with schools, we were very concerned to discover how many safeguarding records were held in filing cabinets stuffed with paper folders. This didn't seem like a secure or practical way of keeping records; apart from anything else, it made it impossible to analyse the data in a proactive way, or to make any sense of it. Brown manila folders, four-ring binders and filing cabinets were (and in many cases still are) the norm. These were sometimes augmented by email and spreadsheets, which are not always any better or even legally compliant.

It seemed unbelievable to us that while some trail-blazing leaders had risen to the safeguarding challenges we've outlined, and moved well beyond basic safeguarding requirements, many schools and colleges were managing safeguarding like a 1950s bureaucracy. At a time when safeguarding challenges have never been more complex, and the legal demands on staff, schools and colleges more stringent, this just doesn't work well enough. You need a system that helps you to be proactive. In fact, you deserve it.

Strategic safeguarding and effective record keeping go hand in hand. Not only because this combination enables you to analyse what you're doing, but also because it empowers you to think beyond the horizon. What would you discover if you could view and analyse your data more easily? Having greater clarity about safeguarding data is one of the primary reasons we created our online safeguarding record-keeping system, MyConcern. We won't be referring to the system much in this book, but from the outset our philosophy has underpinned the development of the system's capabilities and continues to do so.

Over the years, we've seen how many caring and committed people there are working in education who take safeguarding very seriously indeed. We never cease to be impressed by their compassion and dedication, and we're sure you're one of them. However, they're often let down by ineffective systems and processes that create risks that could so easily be avoided. Given the challenges, leaders like you need to work with your head teacher (if that's not you), governing body, and (if you're part of one) your MAT, to develop your safeguarding strategy. You should adopt a perspective that will transform a tactical system into one that integrates governance and leadership, the recording of concerns, effective case management, the secure storage and exchange of sensitive information, and the vital roles of individuals and teams in safeguarding.

To help you with the concepts you'll discover in this book, you can download a strategic assessment tool to fill in as you go along at: https://safeguarding.thesafeguardingcompany.com/assessment-tool. This might sound a bit daunting, but it's not (we promise!). It's just a straightforward way of asking yourself, 'Where are we now, where do we want to get to, and how are we going to get there?' By the time you reach the final chapter, you'll have a ready-made outline strategy, and we think that anything that helps you to save time and be ready for change is a good thing.

Before we dive in, we'd like to add a note on the terminology in this book. When we talk about a 'child' or 'children' we mean people who are not yet 18 years of age, which is the legal definition normally used in the relevant guidance (statutory and otherwise). If we kept chopping back and forth from 'child' to 'young person' or 'young adult', it would become confusing. For similar reasons, we refer mainly to 'pupils' rather than 'students', but again no distinction is to be drawn unless the person is aged 18 or over. In those cases, the students are adults, with different legislation and guidance applying to them if they're vulnerable; some of their legal rights also differ from those of children. That said, the basic principles in this book apply equally to the safeguarding of both children and adults.

A note also on the current context. We refer to 'meetings' and 'meeting' various people, but obviously not all of those meetings are face to face as they probably would have been prior to Covid-19. It will be interesting to see the new working practices that emerge as a consequence of mass vaccinations and the eventual move to a 'new normal'.

And finally, we need to explain that this book is jointly written by both of us – Martin and Mike. However, when we talk about an experience only one of us has had, we switch from 'we' to 'I'. (We've also changed some details to protect the privacy – and sometimes the blushes, both positive and otherwise – of individuals and organisations.) Either way, you're gaining the joint knowledge and insights not only of our experience of safeguarding in education, policing, and many other sectors, but also that of the many talented people we've had the privilege of learning from and working with throughout our professional lives.

Chapter 1
The loneliness of the long-distance safeguarder
Governance, leadership, and management

*I*t was to be a normal software demonstration – or so I thought. *Sue was an experienced secondary school teacher and had been the safeguarding lead for ten years, so when she greeted me warmly at reception I wasn't expecting anything unusual. While I set up, I talked to Sue about the types of safeguarding issues she faced, and her dedication was obvious as she told me about the pupils she'd helped over the years. There was the teenage girl whose stepfather had introduced her to drugs; the 12-year-old boy who'd been bullied because his father had been sent to prison; and the sexting craze that had swept through a group of Year 9 pupils. Sue had patiently and diligently worked with all those young people to keep them safe.*

Once we were ready to start, I was so busy walking her through how the software worked that at first I didn't notice her grow quiet. At one point I asked her a question and didn't receive a reply. Turning from the computer screen to look at her, I saw a single tear making its way down her cheek (the rest she was furiously blinking away). Had it been something I'd said? I looked at her expectantly, encouraging her to explain. Maybe a joke would help: 'Surely the software isn't that bad?' With a choked laugh, Sue took out a tissue and wiped her eyes.

'You don't know how much I've been carrying around in my head,' she said. 'Stuff I've got written in my notebook. Bits of paper and sticky notes that staff hand to me. Snippets of information they tell me in the corridor. Things that wake me up at 3:00 in the morning. It's all there, swirling around. And now, just to know that someone else is concerned about how I do my job and what I worry about – it's such a relief.'

★★★

We share this story to highlight how extraordinarily lonely and stressful the life of a safeguarding lead can be. Just like a long-distance runner, you're on your own. On a wet Wednesday evening, when you're in your car on the way home thinking about how you're going to keep a child safe, it's the isolation that can be the hardest thing to cope with. However, the purpose of this chapter is to show you that you're *not* alone – far from it. In fact, there's a whole structure set up to help you, whether you're making use of it or not. It might not always seem that way, and you might have to take the initiative in using it, but it's there.

The safeguarding arrangements in almost any organisation or setting are made up of three levels of oversight:

1. **Governance:** this is about setting strategic direction, maintaining oversight, and holding leaders to account. In a school or college, governance is usually the responsibility of the governing body; in a private or commercial institution, it could be a board of directors, or a group of trustees in other types of organisation such as a MAT.

2. **Leadership:** this is about creating the right culture and ensuring the right things happen. Leaders are responsible and accountable for the standards of safeguarding, for inspiring others to fulfil their safeguarding responsibilities, and for driving forward improvements in safeguarding policy and practice.

3. **Management:** this is about your day-to-day management of safeguarding and of your team, ensuring that policies, systems, and processes are implemented.

At this stage, we could have a long (and possibly heated) debate about these definitions because inevitably they mean something different in every organisation. However, let's not do that! For the purposes of this book we've used our own simple definitions, which should work well in most contexts.

These three concepts and their associated structures form a hierarchy, and together create a framework for you to work within. To get the best out of this framework you need to understand the roles and responsibilities of each layer, so you can know what to expect of them and how to ask for what you need.

This is important because safeguarding can only work well when it happens in an ordered and strategic way. This involves starting with the end in mind, through planning and personal preparation. When you know what you want to achieve in your school, you'll be able to identify the gaps and barriers that are preventing you from reaching your objectives. You may be motivated by protecting people from harm, or because you're worried about being exposed or criticised, or due to concerns about your organisation being disadvantaged by a high-profile incident. It's unlikely you'll get everything right every day or even be driven only by compassion, because for most people that's not possible. But you do need to be inspired by professional pride and a burning desire to do a proper job. As the safeguarding lead, it's your responsibility to get this right.

Before we go any further, it might be useful for you to take a few minutes to think about the safeguarding mindset in your organisation. The simple matrix below asks you to compare the attitude of certain people or groups towards safeguarding and their level of engagement with it. Put an 'x' on the matrix in a position that best reflects your own safeguarding mindset as the safeguarding lead, and then add an 'x' showing your assessment of the safeguarding mindset of your head teacher (if that's not you), your staff, your governing body or board, your MAT (if you're in one), and your directors or trustees (if you have them).

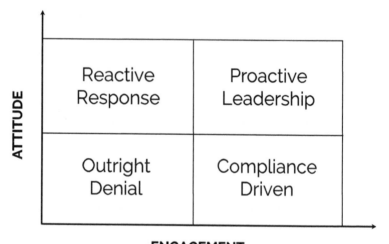

ENGAGEMENT

Figure 2: The safeguarding mindset[1]

Now you've done that, do it again when you've finished this chapter. If any of your x's are not in the same place, and if they're

---

[1] To give some context to the terms used in this model, *Outright Denial* refers to those schools and colleges (and we have met them!) who believe that 'this sort of thing doesn't happen here', while *Compliance Driven* signifies an attitude of simply 'ticking the safeguarding boxes'. In contrast, *Reactive Response* refers to a robust safeguarding regime that deals effectively with concerns as they arise, while *Proactive Leadership* signifies a mindset that maintains a strong reactive response but which is primarily focused on harm prevention and reduction.

not where you think they should be, then what's your plan for putting that right? We hope this book will help you to answer that question, but first let's look in more detail at how the three levels of oversight can help you.

Governance

Your board, governing body, or trustees are there to hold you to account, but also to support you to do a good job. Their role is both strategic and to support people in operational roles. In our experience, safeguarding leads can often have quite a distant relationship with their governors, which isn't the way it should be, so this section is designed to tell you everything you need to know about governance (and possibly were afraid to ask).

In a school, the governing body has three main roles: setting strategy and direction, ensuring the proper use of finance and other resources, and holding the head teacher to account for school performance. If you're interested, the Department for Education has published, and regularly updates, a *Governance Handbook* that sets out the role of governance in schools and MATs in England, along with the statutory requirements.[2] It's a long but really important document.

In summary, the responsibilities of governors and trustees are to:

o carry out their functions with a view to safeguarding and promoting the welfare of children; and
o have regard to the statutory guidance issued by the Secretary of State in considering what arrangements they need to make for the purpose of complying with Section 175 of the Education Act 2002, and the Education (Independent School Standards) Regulations 2014.

---

[2] Department for Education, *Governance Handbook*. Available from www.gov.uk/government/publications/governance-handbook [accessed 17 December 2020].

It's worth noting that the obligations on governors are based in law, and both sets of guidance refer to the responsibilities of governing bodies and proprietors to have effective safeguarding policies and procedures in place.[3] In addition, the government guidance *Keeping Children Safe in Education* 2020 (KCSIE – you'll hear people say this as 'kicksee'), states that:

> Governing bodies and proprietors must ensure that they comply with their duties under legislation. They must have regard to this guidance, ensuring that policies, procedures and training in their schools and colleges are effective and comply with the law at all times.[4]

KCSIE also gives governing bodies and proprietors a specific responsibility to ensure that the school or college contributes to multi-agency working, in line with *Working Together to Safeguard Children*.[5]

Most importantly from your point of view, the *Governance Handbook* also explains that governing bodies and proprietors should ensure the safeguarding lead in a school has:

○ their safeguarding responsibility made explicit in their job description; and
○ the appropriate status, authority, time, funding, training and resources to carry out the role effectively.

---

[3] Across the UK, the various governmental safeguarding requirements apply to both state-maintained and independent schools and colleges, including (in England) academies, academy trusts, and free schools.

[4] Department for Education, *Keeping Children Safe in Education: Statutory Guidance for Schools and Colleges*, September 2020. Available from www.gov.uk/government/publications/keeping-children-safe-in-education [accessed 15 January 2021].

[5] HM Government, *Working Together to Safeguard Children*, 2018. Available from https://assets.publishing.service.gov.uk/government/uploads/system/uploads/attachment_data/file/942454/Working_together_to_safeguard_children_inter_agency_guidance.pdf [accessed 11 January 2021].

Another important requirement is that one of the governors or directors should have specific responsibility for safeguarding. Their job is to ensure proper policies are in place, that relevant systems and processes are working, and that they can see for themselves this is the case. This cascades all the way through the safeguarding hierarchy to frontline individuals, whether they be staff, care workers, teachers or anyone else working with people they are responsible for (including employees and volunteers). In schools and colleges in England, the key responsibilities of the named safeguarding governor are to:[6]

o   keep up with statutory guidance relating to safeguarding and child protection;

o   attend training for named safeguarding governors;

o   ensure the governing board has suitable and up-to-date policies for child protection, staff code of conduct, staff behaviour, and for handling allegations against staff and volunteers;

o   ensure the school has appropriate safeguarding responses to children who go missing from education;

o   ensure the school has appropriate online filters and monitoring systems;

o   report to the full governing board about safeguarding;

o   encourage others to develop their understanding of safeguarding;

o   ensure a Designated Safeguarding Lead (DSL) and appropriate deputies have been appointed;

o   ensure a designated teacher for 'looked after children' has been appointed and trained;

o   meet regularly with the DSL to monitor the school's policy and procedures;

---

[6] The Welsh guidance *Keeping Learners Safe* (Welsh Government, 2020) lists the responsibilities of the Designated Governor for Safeguarding in Welsh schools; see: https://gov.wales/keeping-learners-safe

- ensure all staff, governors and volunteers have been trained appropriately;
- make sure the DSL has sufficient time, resources and training;
- ensure the curriculum covers safeguarding, including online safety; and
- monitor the Single Central Record alongside the DSL to ensure the school carries out the appropriate recruitment checks on staff and trustees.

You can see that the named safeguarding governor has a huge responsibility and one that's crucial to the school or college culture. If they get this wrong, the impact on their school can be catastrophic, whether it be reputational or financial – to say nothing of the effect on the children concerned. And because governors have a financial duty of care, they need to understand that getting safeguarding right in the first place (rather than failing at it and having to face the consequences) is key. The good news is that although the risks are huge, the solutions are not that complex or expensive to put in place. They just need to be implemented systematically.

So what should your governor or director with specific responsibility for safeguarding be doing to support you?

Provide you with the right training

It's not enough for a governor or head teacher to simply say to a member of the senior leadership team: 'Just do safeguarding in addition to your day job – off you go.' Or to include a single line in your job description that says: 'Perform the role of Designated Safeguarding Lead.' How can you know what to do if no one explains or shows you how?

If you're a head teacher in a primary school you're probably also the safeguarding lead, so it goes without saying that the buck stops with you. Do you have the aptitude or experience for the role, or have you been given it because it goes with the headship? And what's in place to give you the information you need to fulfil this part of your job well? A two-hour briefing from your local authority education safeguarding team, together with a set of slides, is hardly adequate.

Give you professional and emotional support

There's often a huge supervision gap among safeguarding leads in education that isn't apparent in other professional roles that deal with safeguarding. In social work and counselling, supervision is a well-trodden path, but it's far less common among school safeguarding staff. For example, a qualified counsellor will have regular compulsory sessions with an experienced therapist (their supervisor). The supervisor's role is to help the counsellor to develop their skills by pointing out what they may have missed and prompting reflection on their approach. Through this, not only do they learn to be more effective but they're also supported emotionally in their demanding work.

You might have people who check you have the right safeguarding policies and processes, but what support do you receive for coping with the fallout from traumatic situations? Supervision should be a basic must-have, not least because as a safeguarding lead you may be working in emotionally fraught conditions on a very regular basis.

Now, here's the thing: many people will not be aware that supervision is already a requirement. In fact, it has been since the latest version of *Working Together* was published in 2018.[7] Unfortunately, relatively few staff in educational settings appear to know about this or have adopted the practice. (Interestingly, a

---

[7] 'Practitioners should be given sufficient time, funding, supervision and support to fulfil their child welfare and safeguarding responsibilities effectively.' HM Government, *Working Together to Safeguard Children*, 2018, p. 56. *Working Together* 'applies in its entirety to all schools' (p. 59). Available from https://assets.publishing.service.gov.uk/government/uploads/system/uploads/attachment_data/file/942454/Working_together_to_safeguard_children_inter_agency_guidance.pdf [accessed 11 January 2021].

reference to the need for safeguarding leads to have 'appropriate supervision' was included in the Department for Education's consultation draft for KCSIE 2020, but it had inexplicably disappeared by the time the final version was published and has not re-appeared in the 2021 KCSIE consultation draft.)

Safeguarding supervision means you have a safe space in which to talk about your most challenging cases and anything else you find difficult. You should feel able to speak freely without any worries about confidentiality. In our view, it should be part of an organisation's duty of care to safeguarding staff, as well as a way of helping to boost your confidence and giving you the chance to reflect on how you've managed things. While some people would benefit from supervision more than others, all safeguarding leads should have it in place as a matter of course, not least for the time when you suddenly need it.

Empower you with the right processes

Your governor with safeguarding responsibility should provide you with access to your governing body or board so you have someone to go to when you have a policy or resourcing issue you can't manage on your own. It might be that you've identified an emerging safeguarding risk that needs policy support from governors, or additional staffing; the issues that come from leaving it unresolved would have serious consequences for pupils, staff, parents, governors, and in some cases the wider community.

In turn, you should ensure that your governors have a good understanding of the current safeguarding issues and risks in your school; they'll want to be reassured that you have a plan to deal with them.

Support you with external agencies

Several hundred thousand referrals are made to children's social care each year, with much of the resulting workload falling on schools to deal with using their own resources. This activity has to come out of budgets that would otherwise be spent on teaching and learning, which is why your governors need to understand the pressure this causes. If you're spending more resources on safeguarding they should be made aware of the impact this could have on teaching capacity.

Also, how does your governing body support you when you refer children to external agencies? As governors ourselves, we've seen how easy it is for local authorities to raise their threshold for intervention due to their own financial pressures. We've sometimes asked our Chair of Governors to spark a debate with the local authority or clinical commissioning group to obtain external support for pupils; you can do this too. Your governors should be asking you how many referrals you're making and to which agencies, whether they're being accepted or rejected and, if rejected, the reasons why.

Making a referral is time consuming and can be difficult, so if your pupils are not receiving the help they need from other agencies and you are unable to make any progress your governors could also be supporting you. For example, with the support of your headteacher your governing body could be engaging with the leaders of those organisations and saying to them:

> In the last x months, we've referred x children to you, and eight out of ten have been rejected. These are children with serious needs and you say they don't meet your threshold. We don't feel sufficient resources are being allocated to this and we'd like to meet you to discuss it.

Your governing body could also contact your local safeguarding partners (previously known as Local Safeguarding Children Boards – LSCBs) on which those agencies are represented, and make the case for the support you need.[8] They'll be more effective if they

---

[8] The statutory safeguarding partners are the local authority, the clinical commissioning group for the area, and the chief officer of police. Schools

do this together with other governing bodies because you can guarantee that other schools are having the same issues as yours. Local authorities in England are under a statutory obligation to safeguard and promote the welfare of children in their area who are in need, by providing services appropriate to those needs. There's no mention in the legislation of this being 'unless there's a period of austerity or the local authority has other priorities'. (This is what we hear all the time from schools.)

Provide enough resources

How much of your school budget is spent on safeguarding? Your named safeguarding governor should know the answer to this. At governing body meetings at one school for which I used to be a governor, we were presented with finance papers that were still warm from the photocopier; this gave us no opportunity to look at them ahead of time so we could understand the figures for ourselves. Governors need to be clear about what's being spent by asking questions and testing things, not to be 'ticking and flicking' through the figures. How on top of the finances are your governors, especially in terms of safeguarding investment?

Related to funding is the increasing need of schools to improve the chances of disadvantaged children. Ofsted's school inspection handbook[9] defines 'disadvantaged children' as those with special

---

and colleges are now considered to be 'relevant agencies' that the statutory safeguarding partners should work with to safeguard children and promote their welfare; in the eyes of many, this 'demotion' from their previous status as a statutory partner within LSCBs was seen as a backward step and potentially damaging to local safeguarding arrangements. The new local partnership arrangements for child safeguarding in England came into effect following the 2016 *Wood Review* (www.gov.uk/government/ publications/wood-review-of-local-safeguarding-children-boards) during a transition period that ran from June 2018 to September 2019.

[9] Ofsted, *School Inspection Handbook*, 2019. Available from www.gov.uk/ government/publications/school-inspection-handbook-eif [accessed 17 December 2020].

educational needs and/or a disability (SEND); those who meet the criteria for Pupil Premium funding;[10] and those in need of help or protection who are in receipt of statutory local authority support from a social worker. The Department for Education specifies that the Pupil Premium is given to pupils who have free school meals (FSM); who are 'looked after children'; or who have ceased to be looked after because of adoption, a special guardianship order, a child arrangements order or a residence order. Safeguarding is an important way of supporting these pupils because disadvantaged children don't tend to do as well as others in their education.

We hope you're starting to feel less alone now, because the role of the governing body is ultimately to support you. You can see you're part of a structure which includes those who hold the financial and policy-making reins of the school, and it's only right that you feel able to play your part in it by asking it for the backup you need. And remember, asking for support is not a sign of weakness; in fact, quite the reverse. It demonstrates your leadership of the issues and your determination to succeed.

However, governance is also there to hold you to account. While this might seem daunting, it's actually a good sign when governors

---

[10] State schools, academies, and free schools in England which have children of service families in school years reception to Year 11 are eligible for Service Pupil Premium (SPP) 'in recognition of the specific challenges children from service families face and as part of the commitment to delivering the armed forces covenant'. Ministry of Defence, 'Service Pupil Premium: What you need to know', updated 4 January 2021. Available from www.gov.uk/government/publications/the-service-pupil-premium/service-pupil-premium-what-you-need-to-know [accessed 15 January 2021]. SPP is currently worth £310 per service child per annum while Pupil Premium, which is targeted at 'disadvantaged children', is worth anything from £935 to £2,300 per child annually. Head teachers with service children in their schools would argue strongly that SPP should be paid at the same rate as Pupil Premium due to the serious disadvantages that services children can face, not least due to frequent school moves.

take an interest in safeguarding because it means they recognise the value of what you do. And yet, ask yourself this: how do they know the safeguarding process in your school is working? Is it purely because you've told them, or because you can *show* them? If they're fulfilling their responsibilities, they should be asking to see evidence of your success; after all, their role is to ensure the effectiveness of your organisation, and no one wants to work in a school or college that can't safeguard children effectively. You only have to look at schools and care homes that have been closed down because of neglect to see what the consequences of poor oversight can be. How you provide evidence of your work is something we'll look at it in more detail in a moment, and later in the book.

Leadership

This is where things become more personal to you because you're the nominated safeguarding lead and you are accountable for the standards of safeguarding in your setting. Your role is to establish the direction, culture and ethos for safeguarding throughout the school, as well as to work out what needs to be done to keep children safe on a day-to-day basis. You may be a busy senior leader such as a head teacher or deputy head, or if you're in a smaller school you may have teaching commitments to manage alongside everything else. Do you have enough time for this? If not, you should make your line manager or named safeguarding governor aware of the problem, particularly if finance is the stumbling block.

This points to an aspect of safeguarding in schools which is, unfortunately, too often unaddressed. It's that safeguarding is often seen as a bolt-on to a teacher's 'day job' without being fully integrated into their workload. The statutory guidance for schools and colleges in England (KCSIE) contains a helpful list of tasks to perform but doesn't identify the personality traits required or the skills needed. There seems to be an assumption that simply being a head teacher, for instance, automatically qualifies you to be an excellent safeguarding lead. We're sure your governors wouldn't appoint someone to any other kind of responsible role without a rigorous selection process, but safeguarding often seems to 'go with the job'.

This means it's up to you to ask the right questions:

o What do I, as the safeguarding lead, need to take personal responsibility for to ensure that I'm capable to perform my role?
o What support do I need, whether it be from my governing body, other members of staff, the local authority, or external agencies?
o Do I know everything I need to know? (You'll never know everything, but you can identify your main knowledge gaps and work out how to fill them.)
o And what about my mindset? Do I have a positive attitude towards learning what I need to know to be able to perform my role really well?
o Am I modelling the approach I'd like other staff to take towards safeguarding?'

This might seem pretty demanding but when you think about it, it's no more than you'd ask of a potential member of staff you were recruiting into a different role.

So what are the key attributes of an effective safeguarding lead?

A strategic mindset

What specific plans have you put in place to ensure effective safeguarding? What objectives have you set yourself? You don't need hundreds of them and they certainly shouldn't be complicated, but if you don't have a clear north star to guide you in your work, you'll end up muddling along in a reactive way. What you need instead is clarity, which is based on both your knowledge of your current situation and the feedback you gain from your governing body, parents, pupils, colleagues and local community.

One way to start is to ask yourself: 'What are the key objectives I want to achieve this year for safeguarding? And how am I going to go about achieving them? Do I have our statutory policies in place? Do people know about them? How can I test if they're working?' Public and private sector organisations have policies galore, but do they make a difference and how do leaders in them know if everyone has read and understood the content? These, by the way, are questions governors should be asking too.

Something we've noticed when working with schools is that although every setting has a school improvement plan, few have a similar plan for safeguarding. But without such a plan safeguarding will inevitably be made up of short-term, tactical measures with no quantifiable objectives, such as educating children on online safety or updating the anti-bullying policy. A more strategic and measurable approach would be, for instance, to devise lesson plans to engage pupils in learning about online safety and to ensure they reach an understanding of it that can be checked. Even better would be to ask them about changes in their behaviour that result from that investment so you can see what's been achieved.

Whatever the initiative, whether it be reducing bullying, preventing drug abuse or alerting young people to the dangers of sexting, if it's in a plan it's clear it will be something you aim to tackle. What's more, if you take your plan to the governors and ask them to invest in it, you're demonstrating leadership. You're also giving them reasons to support and invest in you, because they can see you're taking a strategic and professional approach.

Open-mindedness and professional curiosity

A high level of professional curiosity is important in two ways. Firstly, it helps you to be open to learning whatever it is you need to master your job. This shouldn't be a problem for you – if you've been teaching for many years, you'll probably be the kind of person who's always finding new ways to engage with pupils. You're already an enthusiastic learner.

Secondly, it means you're a better safeguarding lead, because open-mindedness is key to investigating concerns. In our previous lives as senior police officers, we saw first-hand how easy it was for some investigators to make assumptions. In a criminal investigation, for instance, it might have appeared 'obvious' what had happened. However, during our time in the service there was a conscious shift in police training to encourage officers to assume nothing and to be led purely by the evidence. The most dangerous approach was to think, 'I've seen this a thousand times before and I know what's happened here.'[11]

This professional curiosity is also relevant to safeguarding. Is the scenario that's presented to you what's really going on? If a child has a visible injury, for instance, there could be a number of explanations for it, ranging from innocent to criminal. Your willingness to avoid jumping to conclusions should also be mirrored in what you expect of staff, because when people are busy (as school staff always are) they're more likely to make decisions based on what they've seen before. This is probably one of the most serious risks that can affect decision-making in safeguarding.

A knowledge of the needs of the job

Setting the strategy, creating the culture, being self-aware and being honest with yourself about your own abilities are key, as is knowing what support you need to do your job properly.

---

[11] A highly insightful examination of decision-making in child protection and child welfare and the risk of assumptions in the application of 'evidence-based professional practice' can be found in E. Munro, N. Cartwright, J. Hardie, and E. Montuschi, *Improving Child Safety: Deliberation, Judgement and Empirical Research*, 2016. Available from www.dur.ac.uk/resources/chess/ONLINE_ Improvingchildsafety-15_2_17-FINAL.pdf [accessed 3 January 2021].

However, as a minimum you should also be familiar with the relevant statutory guidance for your setting. For instance, in English schools KCSIE contains specific guidance for schools and colleges on the safeguarding responsibilities of governing bodies, senior managers, safeguarding leads, and all members of staff. Similar guidance is in place for schools in Wales, Scotland, and Northern Ireland (links to the relevant guidance in all four UK nations can be found in the Appendix at the end of this book).

A willingness to assert yourself

If you can see that there are gaps in the safeguarding training and experience of your governors, it's your responsibility to help to fill them. The named safeguarding governor should have been on the right training courses, but this doesn't always happen, so you'll need to manage upwards and ask for this to be done.

Part of asserting yourself is also asking for the scrutiny you need from your governing body if you're not receiving it already. Are your governors leaving you alone? If so, that's not a good sign. Being in a position to encourage governors to ask the right questions and to challenge appropriately will help them develop their understanding of your role, and of how safeguarding is managed in your school.

The capacity to delegate

As a leader, learning to delegate effectively is critical (as is knowing when not to delegate). Have a think about what you want other people to do and what you should do yourself. Also, do those people have the skills to undertake what you're asking? The role of the safeguarding lead can sometimes be a lonely one, so working closely with other staff members can improve your decision-making and support you in managing a complex and busy workload.

An ability to nurture professional relationships

Let's face it, you're working in an area in which relationships can sometimes be challenging. You may have to manage difficult conversations with other agencies; you could have a team of deputies to manage; you'll need to work with your school's SEND coordinator; and you may also need to integrate with the work of family liaison officers and counsellors in your organisation. Each of these parties will have their own priorities, which might not always tally with yours. How skilfully you navigate these choppy waters will form a large part of how well safeguarding works in your environment.

There are also parents and pupils to consider when you're working at a strategic level, because your priorities should also be informed by what's important to them. Parents especially are your customer base and, being part of their local community, they probably know more about what's going on there than you. So ask them: 'What are the issues that concern you, related to your child's wellbeing?' There are various methods for doing this. You can create a survey, talk to the parent-teacher association or sit down with a sample group of parents to tease out their concerns. And what about staff? Engaging with people is by far the most effective way of finding out what's concerning them, and you can include representative groups such as 'pupil voice' in this.

This might sound bureaucratic, but it's possible. When we worked in policing, each force had to run several public surveys that would inform their crime prevention strategy. We'd ask questions of victims and motorists who'd been involved in various types of crimes and incidents, and also the wider public. We assumed that people would be most worried about burglary or car crime, so we were surprised to discover that top of their list was cyber crime. When we thought about it, it made sense; burglary and car crime are relatively rare, but for most people the thought of criminals targeting them while they're on their home devices is much more worrying, especially when their children could be targeted too.

Being comfortable with numbers

Financial management and awareness are important. What's the cost of safeguarding in your school? How much of an overhead does the time you spend on it represent? What does it cost to fix a problem as opposed to preventing it in the first place? Imagine your institution has a bullying issue, for instance. Rather than dealing with each incident individually, your safeguarding improvement plan could include preventative work on bullying across a year group, or in a particular section of your school. Through this you could stop many, if not all, of those incidents from happening in the first place, and if you have the figures to back up the success of the approach it will help you in the future. Involving your business manager in identifying the overall cost of safeguarding could be a good first step with this.

An understanding of the key responsibilities of a safeguarding lead

Most of this should be fairly obvious, but it's worth stating your key responsibilities as you won't often see them summarised succinctly in one place.[12] As a safeguarding lead, you are responsible for:

o the way safeguarding is seen and carried out in your organisation;

o managing referrals to external agencies (and internally when appropriate);

o working with others to make sure children are kept safe;

o training yourself and others who need it;

o raising awareness with the right people about the importance of safeguarding and how you want it to work;

o secure and appropriate record keeping (more about that later in the book); and

---

[12] In England, Annex B of KCSIE 2020 contains detailed guidance.

o being available as a centre of expertise and experience for governors and staff.

Safeguarding leadership in a MAT

If you're a safeguarding lead in a MAT in England, you're in a very new role for which there are few precedents and in which you are likely to be responsible for supporting a significant team of safeguarding leads and their deputies across multiple schools. Many of your team – particularly in primary schools – could be head teachers. Also, your schools may span several local authority areas, all with differing child protection and referral arrangements.

Depending on the extent of your responsibilities and the nature of your relationship with your team, you may be required to:

1. prepare and seek approval for MAT-wide safeguarding policies that take into account local authority safeguarding arrangements;
2. represent your MAT in key meetings/discussions with local authorities and other statutory agencies;
3. identify and implement common systems and processes for safeguarding across your MAT;
4. provide safeguarding advice and professional support to your team;
5. supervise the overall casework of your team;
6. monitor safeguarding trends across your MAT to identify issues and risks;
7. manage your team's performance individually in their safeguarding role (this could create tensions for you if some of those are head teachers; how would you overcome this and how would this fit with their current performance management regime with their local governing bodies and your MAT CEO/Executive Headteacher?);
8. arrange for team members to have access to the right emotional support;

9. provide or arrange relevant training and development for your team, school staff and governors and your MAT trustees;

10. ensure that the processes for safer recruitment and the maintenance of the Single Central Record at both a school and a MAT level are appropriate and properly implemented.

And who is going to provide you with support while you do all of this? Your MAT CEO/Executive Headteacher? Your trustees/board? There's a lot for you to think about, plan, and do!

Safeguarding leadership at a MAT level is a significant undertaking and a fast-developing area of professional practice. This is an important opportunity for safeguarding practitioners in education to be recognised for the work that they do and the contribution that they already make, as well as their huge potential to influence multi-agency working and information sharing. There is a perception among many safeguarding leads, often based on their own experiences, of being the 'child' in a 'parent–child' relationship with their local authority rather than being in a genuine partnership and this has to change. MAT safeguarding leads are in a strong position to be the catalysts for that change.

Management

As a safeguarding lead you're not only a leader but also a manager, and that comes with its own set of challenges. You'll almost certainly have a safeguarding deputy, and you might even have a number of people who help you with your responsibilities. In addition, you'll be charged with making sure all members of staff understand how to deal with safeguarding concerns and that they do so effectively.

There are two main areas to focus on here: training and development, and performance management.

Training and development

As a safeguarding lead in a school or college in England, you're required to receive training at least every two years, and as school governors we've been on some of the courses you'll go on. We'd love to say they were positive experiences, but by the end of 63 PowerPoint slides we were exhausted and not much the wiser. Much of the course was a regurgitation of the legislation, and information of little practical value – there was nothing about how to perform the role of safeguarding governor. And lest we forget, governors are unpaid volunteers, often with little or no previous experience of safeguarding and with many other calls on their time, so any governor training needs to be of the very highest quality and should fully equip them for their responsibilities.

Your training can be formal, but more often than not it should be based on developing people's skills by exposing them to different scenarios, or on putting across information in an immersive way. For instance, we carried out some training for a group of schools based on an imagined scenario in which a youngster with a knife had entered the school, hell bent on revenge against another pupil. 'Ah, that's okay,' said the participants. 'We have a lock-down plan.' We agreed that sounded good but wanted to see how it would work in reality. 'Well, we know who the lad is so we'll keep a look out for him, and if he gets into the school we'll ask the head teacher to talk to him.'

'But he has a knife,' we reminded them. 'What will you do about that? And how would you lock down the classrooms? What about communication with all the different members of staff? There's going to be chaos. Pupils will get on their mobile devices to their parents and friends and soon it will be all over social media, so how will you deal with that? And who will call the emergency services?' In this fast-moving situation, responsibilities such as handling the local media, communicating with parents, liaising with the governing body and contacting the emergency services were apparently going to be handled simultaneously by the head teacher in a frantic juggling act. When we pointed out that the head teacher could in fact be the first casualty of this approach, the need for the school to have a critical incident plan became painfully obvious.

Training doesn't have to be dramatic, though. For instance, the last time KCSIE was updated we developed a comprehensive knowledge check, ran some free online training sessions about the changes, and gave the knowledge check to schools to use with their staff. This is an example of a simple tool you can use to make sure people know what they need – it doesn't have to be complex. We will return to the topic of training and development in more detail later in the book in Chapter 6.

Performance management

Although performance management might seem complicated, it's really just about expectations, so it's important to set expectations of staff and measure their performance against them. It goes without saying that everyone who works in your setting should know what their safeguarding responsibilities are, whether they're to report concerns, deal with them, or be proactive about identifying them.

But how do you know whether people are meeting your expectations? And are you even sure what they are? For instance, if some staff never report a concern and others report a lot, what's that telling you? It could be that some teachers are genuinely not coming across any problems, or it could be that they're not switched on to the signs of abuse and neglect. Alternatively, it might be that they're over-reporting because they're not confident about dealing with certain types of issues themselves. If you're managing a large safeguarding team, what performance management systems do you have? And do you have weekly or even daily meetings, and group supervision mechanisms, to ensure consistency of performance?

The value of data

We're rounding off this chapter with the importance of data, because although it may not seem like it at first, it's another part of your support structure. You have your governing body who are there to hold you to account but also to give you the resources you need to do your job well. And you have your team and the other staff in your setting who can work with you. You also have data to back you up so long as you use it properly.

We mentioned earlier how essential it is for your governing body to understand the full picture of the safeguarding situation, and it's part of your role to provide data to show what's happening. Any governor will be keen to ensure their setting is complying with the law and you need to be confident that they're aware of current safeguarding legislation and guidance. You shouldn't find it difficult to gain their attention, because they will be as keen as you are for children to be protected.

So data is an information-passing mechanism, but it's also vital for gaining support for what you do. If you don't have data to bolster your argument that you need more resources to deal with a growing caseload, you'll end up falling back on anecdotes because you don't have the hard evidence. There's also another incentive for good data: if you have great records, you can demonstrate the effectiveness of your safeguarding strategy and your personal contribution.

Data is also essential for tracking trends. For instance, it might show you that behavioural issues are being raised about a particular year group at a higher level than you would expect. Is this something you ought to investigate before it goes any further? What type of issues are they exactly? Do they affect some children more than others? Girls rather than boys? Pupils from black or minority ethnic communities? Those with a particular faith or belief? Students with a physical disability? Or children on Pupil Premium? You need to be able to 'slice and dice' your data so you can see where the issue is raising its head. Given the breadth of contemporary safeguarding issues, you'll inevitably need support from digital safeguarding systems; if you have all your information in paper files stuffed away in a filing cabinet, then you will inevitably be less well-equipped to be proactive.

The simpler the setting, the simpler your system and approach to data can be. The more complex it is, the more your system needs to flex to deal with that complexity. Later on, we'll explore the role of data in more detail, but for now just know it's something you need to systematise in your management role.

Key learning points

- Effective governance, leadership, and management is critical in setting the tone and ensuring a robust safeguarding culture.
- As a safeguarding lead, you have more support available to you than you might realise.
- Your board or governing body is there to hold you to account, but also to support you and to ensure you have sufficient time and resources to perform your role.
- As a leader, you need to think strategically and to have in place well-organised and efficient management systems for safeguarding.
- As a MAT safeguarding lead, you should carefully define your role and communicate your responsibilities to your stakeholders.
- Ensuring comprehensive training and development for yourself and your team is an essential part of your leadership role.

Chapter 2
The safeguarding priority
Planning for prevention

It wasn't long after we started working full time in safeguarding that the Serious Case Review for Daniel Pelka was published. You may recall this tragedy from what you saw in the media at the time, but in case not, Daniel was a four-year-old boy in a 200-pupil school in the West Midlands. In 2012 he died of an acute head injury, and it came to light that for at least six months prior to his death his mother and stepfather had systematically starved, neglected and abused him. The following year, they were both convicted of murder and sentenced to 30 years in prison.

What did this have to do with Daniel's school? From the review, it's clear that although there were failures of communication across several agencies (the school, for instance, had not been told about the parents' history of domestic violence and substance misuse), school staff had failed to spot how serious the situation was. It wasn't as if no one had noticed anything; individual teachers had raised several concerns about Daniel's behaviour and physical state in the months leading up to his death. He was seen by school staff taking food from other children's lunch boxes, and eating food from a waste bin; had visibly lost weight, his attendance was poor, and he had unexplained facial injuries. These issues were discussed both internally and with the boy's parents. However, what compounded the situation was that the school had no systematic way of recording and tracking its concerns, so it wasn't able to identify the overall problem quickly enough. In particular, the plethora of so-called 'low-level' issues weren't picked up as safeguarding red flags; Daniel's overeating (which was how his scavenging for food was interpreted) combined with his weight loss, for example, was seen as a medical problem rather than as a sign of neglect. If the safeguarding lead had been able to see the whole picture, he or she might have been able to intervene at an earlier stage.

Daniel's story gets to the heart of what this chapter is about: the importance of harm prevention. This is an activity you can plan for by developing a robust culture of vigilance in which all concerns, no matter how small, are reported and seen as *part of the whole picture* about a child and their situation. When you become aware of an individual concern, it could appear insignificant – a random element of what could be a more far-reaching scenario. But then comes another concern, and another. You're starting to see a bigger picture emerge, and as the rest of it becomes clear it's obvious that something serious is happening that you need to deal with. It's vital to be able to stand back and analyse the entire situation with a child, rather than only to pay attention to each individual piece of evidence in isolation, because one concern alone may not seem important enough to trigger an intervention.

When we first started researching safeguarding in schools, we found it was common for staff only to report concerns when something serious had happened. In many cases they didn't appreciate the importance of recording relatively 'low-level' concerns and general pastoral issues, which meant that they weren't formally recorded anywhere. This way of thinking has transformed since the Daniel Pelka case, and there's no doubt that schools are recording a lot more than they were in 2012

– particularly the pastoral issues relating to pupils' social and emotional wellbeing. There's also been a noticeable shift in the way that schools encourage all members of staff (and governors) to take safeguarding seriously. This has been supported by subsequent statutory guidance, which has consistently communicated the message that 'safeguarding and promoting the welfare of children is *everyone's* responsibility'.

Schools are also placing a stronger emphasis on the need for staff to spot safeguarding concerns at a much earlier stage than was previously the case. One outcome of this is that safeguarding training is now better focused on the signs and symptoms of abuse, and on the indicators of vulnerability, which may identify a child at risk. This feeds into the concept of seeing the whole picture of a child, because it's not only signs of harm that should make up that picture but also the risk factors in that child's life. While it's impossible for any one person to see the whole situation, it's essential that everyone understands what they should be looking out for and what to do if they have a concern.

Sometimes spotting signs of abuse isn't easy, but by getting to know the children in your setting you'll quickly become aware of any pre-existing concerns and you will be much better placed to identify emerging issues. It goes without saying that if staff and volunteers in your school know a child may be in a difficult situation at home it gives them a head start in spotting a problem. It doesn't mean they have to be overly intrusive, but they may feel it's right to keep a closer eye on the child; this is what we'd describe as being 'professionally curious', and it may include the need for early help.

Early help

The provision of 'early help',[1] or providing support as soon as a problem emerges (or to prevent further ones arising), from

---

[1] In Wales, similar provisions are referred to as 'early support'.

the foundation years through to the teenage years, is a key requirement of *Working Together* and also of KCSIE. As such, it's a concept that you and all staff need to understand.

Early help is a wide-ranging requirement that touches on many aspects of safeguarding. *Working Together to Safeguard Children* specifically requires that practitioners should be alert to the potential need for early help for a child who:

o   is disabled and has specific additional needs;
o   has special educational needs (whether or not they have a statutory Education, Health and Care Plan – EHCP);
o   is a young carer;
o   is showing signs of being drawn into anti-social or criminal behaviour, including gang involvement and association with organised crime groups;
o   frequently goes missing from care or from their home;
o   is at risk of modern slavery, trafficking, or exploitation;
o   is at risk of being radicalised or exploited;
o   is in a family circumstance presenting challenges for the child, such as drug and alcohol misuse, adult mental health issues, and domestic abuse;
o   is misusing drugs or alcohol themselves;
o   has returned home to their family from care; or
o   is a privately fostered child.

So how does early help manifest itself in practice? As a safeguarding lead, it's your responsibility (along with other leaders in the school) to encourage everyone to be as professionally curious as you. Far better for a concern to be raised that turns out to be nothing, than for something critical to be overlooked or ignored. One teacher may not know that their colleagues are reporting their own concerns about the same child, but you as the safeguarding lead can see the whole picture. This aggregated view is what makes the difference between a child's problems going unnoticed and them being given the early help they need. It's also one of the major benefits of an electronic safeguarding recording system because it allows you to see important trends and to monitor problems closely. Even if you don't have such a system for managing concerns, you should at least have something in place which enables you to collect all reports and collate them around individual children.

When it comes to successful safeguarding, it's always a combination of people, systems, processes and leadership that enables your school to stop something bad from happening. Encouraging everyone to speak up is part of leadership. It's worth telling staff that, if they have a concern which they're not sure is serious, they should report it anyway and *you'll* decide. This takes the pressure off them to make a judgement, which is incredibly important because if anyone feels discouraged from voicing their concerns it's a huge risk.

The number-one priority

You'll not be surprised if we say that preventing and reducing harm are the overriding priorities for safeguarding in any educational setting. When investigators look back at the causes of serious incidents, it's usually clear that there were opportunities to prevent them from happening in the first place. We've seen this in numerous case reviews and incident reports. The cost of failing to prevent harm is enormous in terms of the impact on the affected children, their parents and families, their schools, and other children who are connected with them. To say nothing of the effort and resources that are inevitably plunged into repairing the damage.

In recent years this focus on prevention has become increasingly prevalent in many professions. Today, for instance, the police view crime prevention as being just as important as responding to it, if not more so (albeit the police love to respond – it's a great reason to turn on the 'blues and twos'!). Dentistry is another example of improving outcomes through high-quality prevention work. And you'd be hard pressed to find a GP who wouldn't argue that many illnesses treated by the NHS wouldn't occur had their patients adopted healthier lifestyles. The frustration doctors and other agencies have is they don't see people until they have a problem, but teachers have the benefit of interacting with the children in their care on a daily basis. You're on the front line of safeguarding, which is why your school's whole approach should be focused on harm reduction.

It's essential to be proactive in providing early help. If you become aware that a child is in a risky situation it's important that you quickly put in in place measures to protect them before harm occurs or escalates. Being alert to the need for early help is key to preventing and reducing harm.

Safeguarding in context

You may have heard of the term 'contextual safeguarding', which is an important area of growing significance for safeguarding practitioners. Dr Carlene Firmin, a professor at the University of Bedfordshire, has undertaken some ground-breaking work on this topic which has been used to inform working practices in safeguarding (particularly with regard to young people in education). Contextual safeguarding is 'an approach to understanding, and responding to, young people's experiences of significant harm beyond their families'.[2] It takes into account all the relationships a child might build up over time, such as in their communities, at school and online, and recognises that parents can often have little influence over them.

In other words, contextual safeguarding gives you another way of looking at the rich picture around a child that we talked about

---

[2] Contextual Safeguarding Network. Available from https://contextualsafeguarding.org.uk/ [accessed 1 January 2021].

earlier. It allows you to widen your viewpoint to encompass not only what's going on at school (e.g. with their peers) but also who a young person may be associating with in the outside world, online and offline. It might seem like a tall order to be vigilant about activities that are happening outside of your organisation, but we're not implying you should be there to find out, only that you're alert to the signs and symptoms of problems when they make themselves evident.

You can also think about it in a focused way, concentrating on the issues that are most likely to crop up in your school. For instance, the phenomenon of 'County Lines', in which children and other vulnerable people are targeted by organised crime gangs and coerced into supplying drugs, is a growing problem. In 2017–18, Norfolk had the highest number of drug lines of all the counties in the UK. If you were the safeguarding lead at a school in Norfolk, you might identify children who could be vulnerable and think about what you should do to prevent them from being dragged into the scene. You'd be also aware of the indicators that show when a child is at risk. Gangs often buy children gifts in order to groom them, so a Year 10 pupil turning up at school with a new phone and watch, and who seems to have more money than usual, would be a cause for concern. This would be something you could encourage staff to report on so as to build a coherent picture of whether it's an innocent case of a pupil just having had a birthday, or of a vulnerable child being exploited by criminals.

Taking the contextual approach further, you could engage with the police, who may be aware of the local crime gangs and how they operate. One of the strands of your activity might also be to teach pupils about the threat so they're prepared with strategies to resist it. Additionally, you'd work with parents, who may see things at home that you're not aware of.

As you can imagine, the various factors influencing a child's wellbeing exist at different levels in their environment, and they interact in what can often be complex ways. It can feel overwhelming if you think you need to be able to solve all their problems, but the good news is you don't. You just need to know what to look out for so you can share your concerns with the appropriate agencies. The importance of contextual safeguarding is referred to in the KCSIE guidance;[3] it's an area of growing importance and one that's set to become a central plank of harm prevention in the future.

The four principles of harm reduction

At this stage, it's helpful to wrap up this information into a framework. Through our work with schools and other organisations, we've come up with what we call the four principles of harm reduction:

1. Understand the context and identify the risks.
2. Take action to prevent and reduce harm.
3. Develop in children the skills and resilience to avoid, resist and recover from harm.
4. Engage with parents, staff, partner agencies and the wider community to reduce the risk of harm.

We'd like to encourage you to adopt these principles so you can stand a better chance of preventing and reducing harm. Let's look at each of these in turn, and afterwards we'll go through how you can embed these principles into your safeguarding practice by creating an overarching plan.

1. Understand the context and identify the risks

Given that your goal is to prevent harm, you need to understand your school so you know where the main threats to pupils' welfare lie. This will vary greatly from school to school. If yours is a small

---

[3] KCSIE 2020, Paragraph 21 (the term 'contextual safeguarding' was a significant new feature in KCSIE 2019 but the latest guidance has removed the term, albeit it is still referred to in the Ofsted inspection framework).

primary in a rural area, for instance, the problems you're likely to face will be different from those in a large, urban secondary. Some schools may have pupils with links to organised crime, or there could be alcohol issues. If you work in a boarding school, your pastoral concerns will be somewhat different to a day school. It all depends, and taking this into account will enable you to focus your efforts where they're most needed.

Identifying and anticipating harm also comes down to having a high level of professional curiosity, and this goes for individual members of staff as much as it does for you. Curiosity is what encourages everyone to take a concern one step further than they might do otherwise, and to spot the signs and symptoms of abuse or neglect before they've been going on for too long. If a child who's witnessing domestic abuse, for example, would naturally show a different kind of behaviour to one who's taking drugs, then everyone should know what that looks like.

2. Take action to prevent and reduce harm

Despite your best efforts to prevent harm, either by identifying children in need or by joining the dots on small concerns, there will be times when you're faced with reducing the impact of a harmful situation. There are two ways that harm can grow and spread: the first is for an individual child and the second is within a group. In the former, it's a question of noticing changes in behaviour and other signs that all is not well, and then doing something about it before it becomes worse – the same sorts of observations and actions we would advocate to spot the problem in the first place.

However, with a group the situation can be more complicated because issues can proliferate through a cluster of pupils surprisingly quickly. Self-harm is a good example. NHS England figures show the number of girls treated as hospital inpatients after cutting themselves quadrupled between 2005 and 2015, with the number of boys being admitted more than doubling. The causes of this rise are speculative, but include the concept of 'emotional contagion' generated on social media.[4] If you don't identify and deal with this quickly, the harm can proliferate to unmanageable proportions.

It can be easy to assume that if a problem affects a group it will be easier to spot, but you'd be surprised at how this often isn't the case. We recently worked with a safeguarding lead in Dorset who brought up the subject of upskirting, which was made a criminal offence in 2019. 'I never imagined we had a problem with it,' he said. 'In fact, I'd never once come across it at my school. But then a member of staff made a complaint about a pupil upskirting her and when we investigated we discovered it was rife throughout the school – the photos were even being shared on social media. I was horrified.'

This is a great example of how thoroughly investigating one incident, and not assuming it was a one-off, helped to uncover a greater trend which staff were then able to put a stop to. I'm sure you can think of other types of behaviour that go on between pupils such as bullying, harassment and inappropriate online activities, which staff won't necessarily be privy to. Consider how you can put yourself in a position to spot these things.

3. Develop in children the skills and resilience to avoid, resist and recover from harm

The best way of preventing harm is often to help children to avoid it themselves, without the need for adult intervention. This truly nips it in the bud, and enables pupils to develop personal strengths and skills they'll find indispensable in adult life.

---

[4] YOU Magazine, 'What's driving the teenage self-harm epidemic?', 5 August 2018. Available from www.you.co.uk/teenage-self-harm-epidemic [accessed 17 December 2020].

You've almost certainly put in place learning around this already, such as online safety sessions and relationship education. In fact, the teaching of safeguarding in schools is becoming a higher priority than ever before and has now been included in the latest KCSIE guidance. Governing bodies and proprietors must now ensure that children are taught about safeguarding, including online safety. The government also introduced regulations that make Relationships Education (for all primary pupils), Relationships and Sex Education (for all secondary pupils), and Health Education (for all pupils in state-funded schools) mandatory in England from September 2020.[5]

Supporting children to recover from harm when it does occur is even more important now that local authority referral thresholds have been raised. Inevitably, schools end up having to support children who've been assessed as having significant and complex needs, and your school has no doubt felt the impact of this. You need to equip children ahead of time with the emotional resources to recover from harm because it makes sense to educate them to manage their own mental wellbeing. And to be able to do that effectively, you need first to consider your own mental wellbeing and that of your staff (more about which can be found in Chapter 6).

4. Engage with parents, staff, partner agencies and the wider community to reduce the risk of harm

The final principle extends your focus more widely than your school, into your local community and even beyond. This harks back to the contextual safeguarding we explored earlier. It also

[5] Department for Education, *Relationships Education, Relationships and Sex Education (RSE) and Health Education: Statutory Guidance for Governing Bodies, Proprietors, Head Teachers, Principals, Senior Leadership Teams, Teachers*. Last updated 9 July 2020. Available from https://assets.publishing.service.gov.uk/government/uploads/system/uploads/attachment_data/file/908013/Relationships_Education__Relationships_and_Sex_Education__RSE__and_Health_Education.pdf [accessed 17 December 2020].

makes your safeguarding programme more secure because you're approaching it from different angles, and are therefore less likely to miss anything.

When you take a 360-degree approach, you make safeguarding not just about children, or even staff or the school. You make it into a team activity that encompasses parents, caregivers, partner agencies and the wider community. All these people can help to identify and prevent harm before it occurs, and they each have their own perspective. This means that you're not looking at it from only one end of the telescope, and it will help you to formulate a well-rounded, personalised strategy for safeguarding.

Your safeguarding improvement plan

This chapter is all about being proactive, and a key aspect of that is having a plan in place to prevent and reduce harm. We've met some excellent safeguarding leads, and the thing they all have in common is that they're forward-looking in their approach. They understand their settings, they know what the risks and threats might be, and they use this information to put together a strategy to prevent or manage them – which in turn becomes a plan of action. We're sure you've written plenty of plans before so you don't need a lesson from us, but in our experience the best ones are based on SMART principles (specific, measurable, achievable, relevant, and time-based).

Being **Specific** means you understand the context, or current picture of safeguarding in your school and community. This helps you to identify the kinds of issues you need to prevent. In turn, this enables you to set clear objectives which will make your plan focused and tangible.

Measuring how you've dealt with incidents should be pretty straightforward if you have reliable data and can look back over time to see trends. If last year you had a number of self-harm incidents and the majority took place at a particular time of year or in a specific year group, you can put in place a focused plan to counteract them. It's more difficult to evaluate harm prevention because you're trying to measure something that hasn't yet happened. However, you can look at what you would have expected based on the data from previous years, and estimate what would have taken place this time if you hadn't done anything. Something else you can measure is how people feel. Do pupils feel safe (school inspectors will ask them about this)? Do parents think their children are safe (inspectors will ask them this too)? It's important that you know this as well as relying on numerical data from casework.

Achievable plans are, of course, essential as there's little point in planning to do something you can't bring about. Your plan will also help you to be proactive instead of reacting to what happens as you go along. When you're planning ahead, your actions are likely to be better targeted and more effective.

Relevance comes in because your plan is the bedrock of preventing harm. If staff don't feel that the plan is relevant to them, they're unlikely to help you to achieve it. Staff, pupils and parents need to be engaged with it (before it's written), understand its relevance to them, and to feel as if they own the elements in which they can make a difference.

Timeliness in planning is essential. When I was Director of Intelligence in the police, we developed a system of alerts for when a pattern of crimes emerged in an area so we could deal with it before it grew. If household burglaries started to rise in a particular area, for instance, we'd soon know about it because we'd set a trip wire within the system that could alert local patrols. This is why you need a responsive system to work with. Even in a small school it can be confusing for individual members of staff when all they have to go on is, 'Didn't the same thing happen three weeks ago in Year 4?'

To do this you need to establish what's 'normal' and what's a trend. Your 'normal' might be no more than a certain number of bullying incidents in a term (it would obviously be great, albeit unlikely, if normal was zero), so if this starts to increase you can spot it early. You can also set a bar to trigger a response when it's breached. The beauty of this is that you can (to a certain extent) rely on triggers to alert you, giving you time to focus on spotting other problems. Also, you're not being influenced by your own subjective memory and opinions, because it's the data that's doing the talking. You do, however, have to be clear about what 'normal' looks like and your threshold for taking action.

Safer recruitment – the power of deterrence

We'll be exploring safer recruitment and allegations of abuse against adults in more detail later on, but it's worth making the point here that one of the most powerful prevention strategies any school or college can have in place is an effective safer recruitment process that identifies and deters people who may pose a threat to children. Abusers look for opportunities to access children, and will deliberately target and take advantage of those establishments with poor systems and processes. If you have robust procedures, it's far more likely that potential abusers will be deterred or identified.

In his book *Stiff Upper Lip*, Alex Renton recounts his personal experience of sexual abuse at a public boarding school, and interviews other people who have similar stories to tell. What he discovered was truly shocking: that there was complicity between teachers, head teachers and even parents in covering up any potential blight on a school's reputation. This meant that police weren't brought in to investigate and staff were routinely allowed to move between schools, able to perpetuate the abuse still further. You can see the same cover-up culture in businesses and other organisations, where sexual harassment and bullying accusations are hushed up through the use of non-disclosure agreements, and with the result that the abuse continues unchecked.

This shows how, when there's a culture of inaction in a school, it has the consequence of attracting the wrong type of staff and also encouraging the wrong kind of behaviour in children. In contrast, if it's clear to everyone that you have a strong safeguarding culture, and children and staff are encouraged to speak up, this leads to a positive culture right across the board. This is a massive deterrent for potential abusers among staff, but also (far more commonly) for those who might undermine your processes by not complying with them or cutting corners. You've set a standard that people will follow.

An atmosphere of openness, honesty and integrity, combined with a high level of vigilance, always has to come from the leader. We can't emphasise enough how vital this kind of culture is, because not only does it work more effectively it makes your life easier in the long run. It's worth thinking about how much time and effort you spend on this versus firefighting issues when they arise – you might be surprised at the result.

Key learning points

- Preventing and reducing harm is at the heart of safeguarding and is your number-one priority.
- Recording concerns at an early stage is fundamental to taking action at the right time.
- All staff need to know the signs, symptoms, and behaviours in children that may be a cause for concern and how to access early help.
- The principles of harm reduction are: understand the context and identify the risks; take action to prevent and reduce harm; develop in children the skills and resilience to avoid, resist and recover from harm; and

engage with parents, staff, partner agencies and the wider community to reduce the risk of harm.

- The effectiveness of your safeguarding practice will not improve by accident – you will need a safeguarding improvement plan with clear objectives to enable you to track your progress and achievements.
- Safer recruitment processes can be very effective in deterring potential offenders.

Chapter 3
Begin with the end in mind
Recording and case management

*I*was only 19 years old, and a junior police officer, when I first gave evidence in the Crown Court. It was the first time I'd ever been in a court room, and it took me a while to find my bearings in the austere surroundings. I quickly established that the serious-looking chap in the red gown and half-moon glasses was the Judge, and beneath the witness box, within the main body of the court, were several barristers in wigs and black gowns. I had no idea which of them was the defence barrister who would be grilling me. Sitting opposite me were the 12 members of the jury, watching me intently. I smoothed down my uniform tunic, sensing that this was the sort of occasion for which the phrase 'first impressions count' was coined.

I took a deep breath and stepped into the witness box, convinced that I could barely remember my own name, let alone the evidence I was about to give. After taking the oath I just about managed to introduce myself, and waited for the prosecution barrister to emerge from the black-robed throng and ask me the first question. Fortunately, the first two or three were simply to confirm when and where I'd been on duty at a certain time and date, so that was easy, although I had to remember to direct *my responses to the Judge in accordance with my training. Then came an open question: 'Can you describe to the court what happened next?' I knew I'd need to refer to my notebook and asked the Judge for permission, to which he replied, 'And when did you make your notes, officer?' I gave the answer, 'Immediately after the incident, Your Honour.' It was a bit vague but it seemed to satisfy him. An awkward delay ensued as I leafed through my notebook and located the correct page, the court silently watching me all the while. Then I began my account, hoping that my note-taking had been up to scratch.*

★★★

As a safeguarding lead, there's always the possibility that one day you'll be called on to give evidence about an incident you've managed in school. It could be in a criminal court if someone has been accused of committing a crime, or a family court in a child welfare case. Equally, it might be in a disciplinary hearing or an employment tribunal if the matter relates to a member of school staff. Consequently, it's always best to begin working on any of your safeguarding concerns with this in mind, which means recording information in the proper way.

Recording concerns

Effective record keeping is an important aspect of good safeguarding practice and it's essential that members of staff, volunteers and governors all understand how to record and manage concerns. Both the English and Welsh statutory guidance stress the importance of record keeping. In KCSIE 2020, the guidance highlights the need for 'all concerns, discussions and decisions made and the reasons for those decisions' to be recorded. This makes it clear that it's not only the information about the concern that needs to be recorded, but also any other activity carried out by you and your staff. This might include your decision-making process, and the meetings (whether face to face or online) and telephone calls you may have had with various people, including staff, other agencies, pupils and parents.

It is essential that this information is properly recorded, as you may want to refer to it in detail later. What you record can be a vital part of the evidence chain in future proceedings. As a wise Tutor Constable once said to me, 'If it's not written down it didn't happen,' so don't expect the courts, case reviewers or school inspectors to accept your version of events if you haven't recorded sufficient information at the time. This is no theoretical risk: in October 2020, a safeguarding lead emailed me to say, 'I took a call yesterday from the police asking about a family from 1983! There were no records, but I did have some information in my head.' One element of record keeping that can be hard to judge is what kind of language to use. You should keep your information factual, and include any relevant details such as the evidence for your concerns. Avoid personal assumptions and judgements, such as 'having a feeling' that something isn't right. It's fine to have that feeling, by the way, but there's always a reason why you feel like that – try and identify what it is. Also, use professional language that's easy to understand and steer clear of expressing opinions (for example, we've encountered school staff wanting to record 'poor parenting' as the reason for a child experiencing a particular safeguarding issue). The local threshold guidance that we referred to earlier can be a helpful source of professional terminology.

Also, when we train safeguarding leads we always ask them to think about where their words might end up. Would you feel comfortable with them being read out in court, for instance? A good way of approaching record keeping is to remember 'the five WH': Who, What, When, Where, Why and How (these will already be familiar to many teaching staff). When you've recorded or reviewed the facts using these headings, you can ask yourself the question 'so what?' to help you decide on the appropriate course of action.

Here are our ten top tips for record keeping that will help you to demonstrate your thinking and make clear the justification for your decisions:

1. Use clear, straightforward language and be concise.
2. Avoid jargon and technical language whenever possible.
3. Differentiate between facts, opinions and professional judgements.
4. Include all relevant information, even if it appears contradictory.
5. Record your decisions *and* the rationale for those decisions, as well as the other options you considered (if any) and why you ruled them out.
6. Use the child's words if they've made a disclosure.
7. Record the details of any contact or attempted contact (however minor) with other agencies or key people, including parents and caregivers.
8. When sharing information, record why, what, when, how and with whom.
9. If you decide to share information without consent, or *not* to share information, record the reasons why.
10. Record a summary of the outcome of the case and who you've informed about it.

Less serious concerns

The recording (or not recording) of less serious concerns has featured prominently in many case reviews, and this is where education staff have sometimes been criticised for overlooking the signs and symptoms of abuse. So you can see why making a note of anything that's worrying, even if it seems like a small matter, is integral to good safeguarding. Let's start with the basics. What should you record and why?

Firstly, everyone in your organisation needs to know what the threshold is for recording a concern. As we mentioned in the previous chapter, a historical problem has been that people don't always know what they should record, resulting in safeguarding leads having gaps in their understanding of a risk. You therefore need a clear policy on this. Many local safeguarding partnerships provide guidance about thresholds, and set out the types of information you should record and include in referrals.[1]

Secondly, everyone needs to know what they're looking for in the first place, and this will vary between settings. If a child at your school has behavioural issues, at what point do you record that as a safeguarding concern? If they're normally well behaved but you notice a change over a few days, is that something to worry about? Or maybe they were outgoing before and have now become withdrawn. People need to know where to draw the line (and the threshold can be low).

Part of the decision-making process is being aware of any pre-existing concerns about the child, especially if they're vulnerable, if they've already been designated as being 'in need', or if they're part of a group in which contextual safeguarding would come into play. That said, although it's important to have guidelines for staff to follow, you should also make it clear that they're free to use their own judgement if something doesn't seem right to them. Your message should be: 'If in doubt record it.'

You also need a procedure for reporting by third parties such as school taxi and bus drivers. And if your school or college receptionist was to pick up the phone to an anonymous caller who had information about a child, would they know what to do?

---

[1] Suffolk Safeguarding Partnership, 'Threshold document and guidance'. Available from https://suffolksp.org.uk/safeguarding-topics/childrens-topics/threshold-document-and-guidance/ [accessed 17 December 2020].

Complex cases

Clearly there's a difference between making a simple observation about a child and the kind of record keeping required for more complex cases. But first, let's consider the many reasons for keeping organised and thorough notes in complicated situations.

○ You have a clear chronological record of what happened and when, and who took what action and why, so you can track what's been said and done.

○ You've recorded your basis for decision-making; it's important to record not only what you did but also what you decided *not* to do, and why.

○ You can demonstrate to children, parents and caregivers the action that you've taken to safeguard your pupils (in England, children aged 12 and over are deemed by the Information Commissioner to be competent to make a subject access request on their own behalf, so unless one of the legal exemptions applies they can legitimately ask to see what you've written about them).

○ Internal staff and external agencies can see the information they legitimately need.

○ Records help you to refresh your memory, which is especially important if the case has been going on for a while or you need to hand it over to someone else.

○ The records can be transferred to a new school if the child moves.

○ You'll need access to the records if you have to give evidence in legal proceedings or present information in a case conference.

○ They help to protect you and your staff from unfounded allegations of inaction or misconduct, as well as from legal proceedings, which could all have professional and financial consequences for you and your school.

○ They provide evidence for Ofsted, Estyn, the Independent Schools Inspectorate (ISI) and other reviews.

o   The act of making records helps you to keep a clear head when it comes to managing emotional and stressful situations.

o   The records demonstrate that you have a culture of safeguarding and that the protection and safety of children is your top priority.

You may wonder why it's important to record the reasons for your actions, as well as the actions themselves. It's so that you can explain them later if you need to. Although it's unlikely you'd be called upon to give evidence in court, you might have to justify yourself internally or to external agencies, and it's incredibly helpful if you can refer to your records for this. When we've given evidence in court as police officers, we've often been asked about our thinking process; for example, 'Why did you choose to take this option? Why did you decide to share that information with that person?' When you're under pressure the last thing you need is the added burden of not being able to remember why you did something. Complex cases are full of tricky decisions, which probably means that there was more than one course of action you could have taken, so it's worth recording what those were and why you decided not to pursue them.

On a separate but related note, for several years there's been an ongoing (and sometimes heated) debate in the UK about the controversial topic of mandatory reporting. It's been examined in detail by the Independent Inquiry into Child Sexual Abuse (IICSA), but the inquiry has yet to deliver a final view.[2] Back in the 1960s, the United States introduced the mandatory reporting of child sexual abuse concerns, and

---

[2] Independent Inquiry into Child Sexual Abuse, *Mandatory Reporting Seminar 1 – Existing Obligations to Report Child Sexual Abuse: A Summary Report*, December 2018. Available from www.iicsa.org.uk/key-documents/8725/view/mandatory-reporting-seminar-one-summary-report.pdf [accessed 17 December 2020].

similar provisions were later enacted in Canada and Australia. Mandatory reporting places a legal duty on certain people, sometimes parents but more often staff in statutory agencies (including education), to report any relevant concerns to certain public bodies such as children's services or the police. In the UK, statutory reporting requirements currently apply to teachers in relation to female genital mutilation (FGM)[3] and the prevention of terrorist radicalisation (known as the Prevent Duty[4]).

In England, there's currently no blanket mandatory reporting requirement and it's often argued that existing statutory guidance and professional obligations are sufficient. In Wales, the Social Services and Well-being (Wales) Act 2014 placed a legal duty on certain groups of professionals to report a 'child at risk' to the local authority. Mandated groups included local authority staff, police, probation and offender services including youth offending, health staff working for local health boards and NHS trusts, and those discharging their functions under the Learning and Skills Act 2000. That legal duty arose from concerns relating to historic abuse,[5] with the principle being that reporting should not be a matter of personal choice; a recommendation was made by an expert ministerial Safeguarding Advisory Panel that the expectation to report should be strengthened to a duty. The duty in Wales is 'to report "concerns" rather than "known facts" because evidence of harm might not always be present'. However, there's no specific penalty for a professional in Wales failing to report their concerns, as 'any failure of a professional to report concerns is dealt with through agencies' own existing fitness to practise and internal disciplinary processes, and referral to professional

---

[3] Introduced by the Serious Crime Act 2015.

[4] The Prevent Duty was introduced by Section 26 of the Counter-Terrorism and Security Act 2015.

[5] Sometimes referred to as 'non-recent abuse'.

regulators'.[6] So while in the majority of instances the reporting of safeguarding cases is currently not compulsory across the UK, it might be in the future.

Your recording system

Now you understand what it means to record information about a case, where do you record it and how do you store the data in the long term? What system do you use – paper records, spreadsheets, a bespoke safeguarding case management system or something else? There are a number of options, so it's worth considering the features of a system that's fit for purpose. In our experience, this is what it should be or do.

Be accessible by all staff

It should be easy for any member of staff to access the system so they can record a concern without difficulty or delay. It doesn't mean they have to manage the case themselves (the safeguarding lead can triage it and respond if necessary), but it's essential that anyone from a receptionist to the head teacher can use it with ease. There should be no barriers, either practical or psychological, to the recording of concerns.

Professionalise its users

It should be easy to enter the right information in the right way. An electronic system can be set up so that it guides people through the process, enabling them to be competent reporters,

---

[6] Independent Inquiry into Child Sexual Abuse, *Mandatory Reporting Seminar 1 – Existing Obligations to Report Child Sexual Abuse: A Summary Report*, December 2018, p. 4. Available from www.iicsa.org.uk/key-documents/8725/view/mandatory-reporting-seminar-one-summary-report.pdf [accessed 17 December 2020].

working in line with best practice and legislation even if they've not used it before. For instance, a good system will remind users to enter information in a specific way, ensuring that it's recorded consistently. This can be a great help to you when you come to collate it for review; the last thing you need is quirky, individualistic record keeping.

Of course, it doesn't need to be an online system for it to work like this – a paper-based system could also fill this requirement. However, paper-based systems are becoming increasingly impractical due to the operational and legal requirements of safeguarding. For instance, the Covid-19 pandemic and the responsibility for all schools and colleges to undertake remote (off-site) or hybrid (both on- and off-site) safeguarding has brought into stark relief the limitations of paper systems.

Chronologise the data

When formal proceedings are underway, it's the chronology of events that external agencies and the legal profession rely upon. This means that the chronology is a key feature of an effective safeguarding system, and is the place where you record the main events linked to the case you're managing. This could include updates, key decisions, relevant meetings and interactions, and risk assessments.

It's a lot of work to prepare a chronology of events for a case conference or in legal proceedings, and it can be a daunting experience if you rely on a paper-based system. We've met quite a few safeguarding leads who've described spending their weekends trying to organise paper records into meaningful chronologies, which is why your safeguarding system should be capable of processing the data into time frames. Of course, it's not only the case chronology that's important but also the chronology for an individual child; you might need to see all the relevant information about a pupil recorded as a history from 'Day One'.

If you don't have this kind of aggregated view, you won't be able to produce the relevant background information or an accurate sequence of events.

You should also be able to redact your chronologies when you need to, which is often the case prior to formal legal proceedings; for instance, masking information about other people referred to but who aren't relevant to the case. Ideally your system should allow you to redact words easily (we still often hear about safeguarding leads having to use black felt-tipped pens for this). It's important to remember that 'redaction' does not mean 'deletion' – redaction is the ability to obscure sensitive data for legal or security purposes; it does not mean altering or deleting original records. We believe that having the ability to edit or delete records in any safeguarding recording system, particularly entries in a chronology, is potentially a very dangerous practice if there are no proper audit trails. Those records may well be required in legal or other proceedings and there have been a number of notorious cases where records have been altered by social workers and police officers, either to save their own embarrassment because of poor professional practice or to skew evidence.[7] In some instances, this has resulted in the imprisonment of those concerned. Consequently, it is very important to ensure that staff are well trained in record keeping and understand these issues. (We go into much more detail about information management in Chapter 5.)

---

[7] We regularly speak to safeguarding leads who are worried about the language used by staff when recording concerns because it is 'unprofessional' or because what the staff member has recorded is incorrect. Staff training is by far the best way of avoiding these issues and ensuring that safeguarding records contain appropriate language and content. However, if mistakes are made it's far better to make a subsequent entry pointing this out and providing the correct information rather than trying to erase the original entry. In our extensive experience of giving evidence in legal proceedings it was always more convincing to present records that were 'imperfect', rather than pristine records where no one had ever made a mistake or recorded something in haste that with hindsight proved not to be correct.

Cross-reference data between children and cases

This is where your system comes into its own with case management. You need to have a way of linking concerns to the children involved, and to other children and agencies connected with them. Suppose you had four children involved in a safeguarding incident; with an online recording system you could direct the data into each of the individual profiles (their personal case files) from a single report, so whichever profile you were looking at would show you the three other children involved. If you had to do the same with a paper-based system it would be a soul-destroying bureaucratic pain! Another great advantage of an electronic recording system is its ability to integrate with your other IT systems, such as school and colleges' Management Information Systems. This can massively reduce bureaucracy and enable much greater opportunities for cross-data analysis, as well as maximising on the investment you have already made in those other systems.

Create effective audit trails

An audit trail protects the system (and you) by recording the fact that records have been added to, altered or deleted. A paper system is particularly fallible because the content of the documents can be changed and there's no automatic way of knowing if that's happened. Also, paper can be lost, destroyed or damaged, and is only physically available to the person who has it in their hands (unless it's copied and distributed, in which case you've lost control of the information). A real-life example of the problems this can cause is when a social worker from Somerset doctored paper records over a six-week period by recording five visits that hadn't taken place. Forensic experts uncovered her activities and she was struck off the register.

You may wonder what you'd do if someone made a mistake on an electronic system, such as entering information into the wrong field, and couldn't delete it because of the safety systems in place. In practical terms it's not a problem – all they have to do is record the error and what they've done to put it right. It may be mildly inconvenient, but it's a small price to pay for being secure in the knowledge that your safeguarding records are reliable. Having an audit trail is designed to deter people from misusing systems, not to penalise people who make genuine mistakes.

Case management

The concept of case management is something you often hear social workers or the police talking about, but it may seem a bit foreign to you as someone working in education. So what is it? According to the Case Management Society UK, it's 'a collaborative process which assesses, plans, implements, co-ordinates, monitors and evaluates the options and services required to meet an individual's health, social care, educational and employment needs, using communication and available resources to promote quality, cost-effective outcomes'.[8] While this definition has been used primarily for health and social care services, its principles are just as applicable for safeguarding in education.

In simple terms, case management is akin to project management. You have a concerning situation involving a vulnerable person that you want to resolve, legitimate reasons for wanting to resolve it, and a plan for how you're going to do so and who should be involved. You also have a need to record all the decisions and actions related to it for future reference.

As with all projects, your cases will involve other people as well as yourself. This is essential, because if you don't share information

---

[8] Case Management Society UK, 'What is case management?'. Available from www.cmsuk.org/case-management/what-is-case-management [accessed 17 December 2020].

or involve others at the right time, relevant members of staff will be operating in the dark. The most effective safeguarding leads are those who bring in others and delegate appropriately. Apart from anything else, it's important that if you're not around for some reason someone else knows what's going on with a child. We've seen safeguarding leads go off sick, for instance, and the class teachers of the children concerned not being aware of concerns about them.

Involving other members of staff doesn't have to be a formal affair; you could include them in a monitoring capacity if you like. If you approach a member of staff and simply say, 'You need to be aware we have some concerns about this child and we'd like you to keep a close eye on them,' this can often be all that's needed. The staff member will appreciate having the opportunity to contribute, and you can even put a small team around a case to help you (or to manage it on your behalf). You don't have to do everything on your own, although you do need to ensure you can justify your decision to bring someone else on board.

If you're concerned about data protection, the law says that protecting a child is a legitimate reason to share information with another member of staff or with external agencies. It might be that you've identified a child in need and have referred them to another agency, and now there's a joint plan in place to manage the issue. The right people in the school have a clear role to play in conjunction with those agencies (we'll be talking about working with external people more fully in the next chapter).

Depending on the size of the setting you work in, you may also have a range of specialists you can bring in to help you, such as counsellors, school nurses and family liaison officers. Generally, you should give them as much information as you can to help them fulfil their role, including inviting them into the chronologies of your cases. It's important that they have a full picture of the risks surrounding a particular family or child.

One of the major case management dilemmas a safeguarding lead has to cope with is whether or not to refer a child to another agency, which will probably be the local authority department called 'children's social care' (sometimes referred to as 'social services'). This can pose a genuine quandary: you don't want an otherwise manageable situation to spiral out of control, but neither do you want to delay bringing in child protection experts in a timely manner. It can be difficult to know when to share and not to share information. This is when it's incredibly helpful to seek advice at an early stage, and you can gain informal feedback from social care without making an official referral.

Handling conversations with parents is one of the most challenging things you have to do as a safeguarding lead, especially if the family has complex needs. As school governors we've experienced this first-hand when we've met with angry and distraught parents who had complained about the way their child's safeguarding case was being handled. For teaching staff with limited training and no legal background, these conversations can be doubly difficult to deal with, especially if you're managing a case at the more serious end of safeguarding. So having a plan about what you'll tell the parents (or not tell them if there would be safeguarding risks in doing so) is essential, particularly if one of them is an alleged perpetrator. In these situations it's really important to work closely with other agencies.

Managing disclosures

If you've been in an educational setting for a while you may have been the recipient of a serious disclosure from a child. There's probably nothing that can prepare you for the moment when a pupil tells you they've been abused, neglected or harmed in some way – it's a stressful and emotional experience for both of you.

That's why it's helpful to know what to do ahead of time, so that you're able to handle things professionally and record the right information.

Your natural response if this happens might be to grab a pen and paper so you can make notes while the child is talking to you, especially if you know that recording their actual words is important. However, your focus first should be on demonstrating to that child that you are listening and acknowledging their immediate concerns without asking leading questions, and then responding appropriately to what they have to say.

There are several excellent resources produced by the NSPCC's *Let Children Know You're Listening* project,[9] which will help you with this. Representatives from the charity gave a presentation at one of our conferences, which the safeguarding leads there found extremely helpful because although they (like you) receive advice on what to record and how, there's quite a skill in taking a disclosure and knowing how to interact with a child in that moment. The NSPCC has produced a poster and an animation[10] that you can download for your own school, and which summarises three key tips to follow:

1. **Show you care, help them to open up.** Give your full attention to the child or young person and keep your body language open and encouraging. Be compassionate, be understanding, and reassure them their feelings are important. Phrases like 'you've shown such courage today' help.
2. **Take your time, slow down.** Respect pauses and don't interrupt the child – let them go at their own pace. Recognise and respond to their body language. And remember that

---

[9] H. Baker, P. Miller, E. Starr, S. Witcombe-Hayes, and C. Gwilym, *Let Children Know You're Listening: The Importance of an Adult's Interpersonal Skills in Helping to Improve a Child's Experience of Disclosure.* NSPCC, 2019.

[10] NSPCC, 'Let children know you're listening'. Available from https://learning.nspcc.org.uk/research-resources/2019/let-children-know-you-re-listening [accessed 17 December 2020].

it may take several conversations for them to share what's happened to them.

3. **Show you understand, reflect back.** Make it clear you're interested in what the child is telling you. Reflect back what they've said to check your understanding – and use their language to show it's their experience.

Case managing a critical incident

Here we're going to look at the management of critical incidents in your setting, and the issues you need to think about when dealing with serious and complex safeguarding concerns. But first, what is a critical incident? A useful definition might be:

> A critical incident is any incident where the effectiveness of the school or college's response is likely to have a significant impact on:
>
> o the safety or wellbeing of the victim or any other person; and/or
> o the confidence of the victim, other pupils, their families, staff, stakeholders, and/or the wider community.[11]

Consider, for instance, a pupil making an allegation of a criminal nature against another pupil, or even a member of staff. The reason these are so tricky to manage is that the accuser and alleged perpetrator study or work in the same environment.

In recent years, we've seen a significant increase in the number of reports of peer-on-peer abuse and harmful sexual behaviour in schools. Not only has the volume of concerns increased but so has the severity of them, with serious sexual assaults (including rape) being reported more frequently. This has created issues for schools when they're thinking about how to manage the needs of

---

[11] This is based on the police definition of a critical incident that has been specially adapted for safeguarding in educational settings.

both victims and alleged perpetrators, especially if they're in the same class or year group. The temptation is to focus on removing the child who's been accused, but if this isn't handled sensitively it could cause problems if any concerns about the truth of the allegation arise later on. On the other hand, what should you say to a parent who's outraged that their daughter, for instance, is having to sit in lessons with the boy who is accused of assaulting her?

Obviously, if a sexual assault has taken place your first action is to inform the police, but it's how you manage the fallout from the allegation and the dynamics of the situation that will greatly influence what happens next. At some point you may have to find a way of separating the pupils within the school, which might not be an easy thing to do. You also need to factor in witnesses and how you're going to manage their contact with both parties. You need to be balanced in your approach.

Here's a summary of the key factors you need to consider when dealing with a serious and complex case involving sexual violence or harassment between pupils.[12]

o   Reports of sexual violence and harassment are likely to be complex and require difficult professional decision-making, often quickly and under pressure. You need to be prepared for this and to understand the guidance and relevant policies in your area.

o   Make sure your staff are trained to take a disclosure; they should know what to do when an incident occurs. This is because the quality of the initial response to a serious sexual assault is critical for preserving evidence and supporting the victim.

o   Effective policies and procedures provide you with the foundation for a calm, considered and appropriate response.

---

[12] The key points have been taken from the relevant guidance in both England (*Keeping Children Safe in Education* 2020) and Wales (*Keeping Learners Safe* 2020).

o It's essential that you reassure the victim they're being taken seriously and that they'll be supported and kept safe. A victim should never have the impression that they're creating a problem by reporting sexual violence or harassment, nor should they be made to feel ashamed about it.

Effective safeguarding practice includes:

o not promising confidentiality at the initial stage, as it's likely a concern will have to be shared further;

o recognising that a child is likely to disclose to someone they trust, who could be anyone on the school or college staff;

o listening carefully to the child, being non-judgemental, being clear about boundaries and how the report will be progressed, not asking leading questions, and only prompting the child where necessary with open questions such as where, when and what;

o considering the best way to make a record of the disclosure (best practice is to wait until the end of the disclosure and immediately write up a thorough summary, which allows you to devote your full attention to the child);

o only recording the facts as the child presents them (your notes shouldn't reflect your personal opinion), as the resulting report could become part of an assessment by children's social care or a criminal investigation;

o if possible, managing reports with two members of staff present (with one of them preferably being the safeguarding lead or a deputy);

o informing the safeguarding lead (or deputy) as soon as practically possible if they're not involved in the initial report; and

o carrying out a risk assessment that takes into account the needs of the victim, the alleged perpetrator, and all other children at the school (it's worth preparing one of these in advance so you can add details to it if the worst happens – you'll be glad you were ready for it).

A note on evidence (you can tell we're ex-police officers): it's important to collect it and preserve it well. If there's been a serious sexual assault, evidence could be on clothing, for instance. You need to ensure there's no cross-contamination between the victim and alleged perpetrator, so keep the pupils apart. Also, if you or other staff members have contact with the victim as part of your initial response, bear in mind that you won't be the right person to talk to the other party as you could unwittingly transfer forensic evidence onto them. Of course, you're not a trained crime scene investigator and nor are you expected to be, but these are some simple and sensible precautions you can take.

Recording marks and injuries

If a member of school or college staff spots an injury on a pupil,[13] they need to ask how it was caused and to record the details.[14] A method widely used in many professions is for marks and injuries to be drawn onto a body map. There are a range of age-appropriate body maps in use, covering babies, children and adults; until relatively recently these were all paper based, but now they can be found in a safeguarding software system such as MyConcern. During our policing careers, body maps were routinely used by pathologists at post-mortems, by social workers recording injuries observed on children, by police surgeons attending police stations to examine victims and detainees, and by paediatricians examining child victims.

Surprisingly, the recording of marks and injuries seen on a child by staff in schools and colleges is a topic on which government guidance is largely silent. The use of body maps for safeguarding

---

[13] Any definition of 'injury' should include minor marks and abrasions as well as bruises, cuts, and more serious injuries.

[14] Even if a victim states that an injury is accidental, it's still important to record it. Injuries claimed by a victim to be accidental are regularly found to be non-accidental.

in education appears to have grown out of their use in other professions and without any central policy initiative (indeed, many of the templates in use seem to come from the same sources, and look like they were drawn in the 1950s). In 2017, we sent a Freedom of Information request to all local authorities in England and Wales, asking whether they recommended the use of body maps and digital photography for recording marks and injuries in relation to safeguarding in schools. Of the 149 local authorities that responded, only 26% even had a policy (and even fewer, only 15%, had a policy on the use of digital photography to record marks and injuries).

This leaves school and college staff in a difficult position. Should they be using body maps to record marks and injuries? Local authorities appear to be evenly divided on this issue, with some believing they're essential and others viewing them as unnecessary and possibly even dangerous, as they could implicitly 'authorise' the physical examination of children by school staff. In some settings (particularly in special needs education), staff will be administering intimate or personal care to pupils, and they'll inevitably observe marks and injuries on intimate parts of a child's body. These may have many causes, including medical conditions or from equipment used to assist a child. But if, for example, a member of staff in a primary school observes a visible injury on a clothed child, should they remove clothing to look for other injuries? Our view is absolutely not, but where is the policy guidance that makes it clear? Our contention is that a child should only be examined for injuries by medical professionals in an appropriate setting. Other than in a medical emergency, the necessity for such an examination should be decided by children's social care or the police.

We believe there's an urgent need for national policy guidance on the use of body maps in schools and colleges, and for the investigation of marks and injuries. It's a complex area, and there must be absolute clarity for safeguarding practitioners.

Allegations of abuse against adults in schools and colleges

KCSIE states that the guidance should be followed when it's alleged that a teacher or another member of staff (including supply staff and volunteers) has:

o   behaved in a way that has harmed a child, or may have harmed a child;
o   possibly committed a criminal offence against or related to a child;
o   behaved towards a child or children in a way that indicates he or she may pose a risk of harm to children; or
o   behaved or may have behaved in a way that indicates they may not be suitable to work with children.[15]

It's worth noting that the guidance doesn't specify that the child has to be a pupil; it could be any child. The head teacher would normally take the lead on such allegations as there are strict protocols to observe. If the allegation is against the head teacher, it must be reported to the Chair of Governors (or Management Committee in an independent school). However, in many schools, especially primary schools, the safeguarding lead and the head are one and the same person, so we'll go through the main points to consider.

As with all serious allegations, it's important to stay calm and to take a sensitive and balanced approach. Your first focus is to ensure that any victims are protected from further harm and properly supported. You should also preserve any evidence as quickly as possible, because a guilty perpetrator will inevitably try to destroy it. This could include physical evidence such as clothing, documents or school records. Of course, if it's a criminal allegation the case management of it will be taken out of your hands as soon as you report it to the police, but you'll

---

[15]   KCSIE 2020, Paragraph 211, p. 56.

still need to manage the consequences of the incident internally. Simply 'getting rid' of a staff member or volunteer, or cancelling the contract for a supply teacher, will do nothing to prevent them working with children elsewhere and you have no idea of the risks they might already be posing to other children outside your school.

You should apply careful judgement when dealing with allegations against an adult. Some cases won't warrant a police investigation or further enquiries by children's social care, but the Local Authority Designated Officer (LADO)[16] has an important role to play in deciding on a course of action (in collaboration with you, social care and the police). If, after you've carried out an initial evaluation, you establish that the allegation is unfounded, you should record this fact along with your grounds for reaching that conclusion. You should then consider what action you need to take in respect of the person who made the allegation.

In all of this you need to be discreet because the school has a duty of care towards the adults working there and should provide appropriate support to those who are the subject of allegations. It can be traumatic for the person concerned as well as their family, particularly when allegations prove to be unfounded. It's important that you maintain confidentiality and guard against any unwanted publicity while the allegation is being investigated. Legislation makes clear that 'publication' of material which may lead to the identification of the teacher involved is prohibited. This means, for instance, that a parent who posts details of the allegation on social media is in breach of the law if what they've written could lead to the public identification of the teacher.

---

16 It is a statutory requirement for every local authority in England and Wales to appoint a LADO, who is responsible for coordinating the response to concerns that an adult who works with children may have caused them or could cause them harm.

Dealing with allegations of abuse against adults is rarely straightforward and many schools can find it challenging, especially as these events come along infrequently. In February 2020 the Department for Education published its research on this topic.[17] The research examined schools' approaches when dealing with allegations against adults, and highlights both a lack of practical experience in evidence gathering and the variable levels of support available to safeguarding leads and head teachers. It also reported on the inconsistent approaches between schools when dealing with allegations, thereby emphasising the need for effective training and support on this important subject.

Whistleblowing: Case study – Nigel Leat

A separate but related issue for safeguarding leads is that of whistleblowing. A common feature of many of the cases when teaching staff have sexually abused pupils is that other staff had seen and heard things that they could (and should) have reported to the head teacher, the safeguarding lead or the LADO. This could have identified an offender at a much earlier stage. A prime example of this is the case of Nigel Leat, a teacher in a small school in North Somerset where he taught for 15 years.[18] In May 2011, Leat pleaded guilty to 36 offences against pupils there. The charges included one count of attempted rape, 22 of sexually assaulting a child under 13, and eight of sexual assault by penetration, all involving young girls between six and eight

---

[17] Department for Education, *Research on the Use of Part 4 of Keeping Children Safe in Education Guidance*, February 2020. Available from https://assets.publishing.service.gov.uk/government/uploads/system/uploads/attachment_data/file/867935/KCSIE_part_4_research_report.pdf [accessed 17 December 2020].

[18] North Somerset Safeguarding Children Board (NSSCB), *Serious Case Review: The Sexual Abuse of Pupils in a First School Overview Report*, 25 January 2012. Available from www.northsomersetsafeguarding.co.uk/userfiles/downloads/182/283.pdf [accessed 11 January 2021].

years of age. Leat's offending took place in his classroom and he actually filmed some of the offences he committed. During the investigation it transpired that there were at least 30 incidents witnessed by other members of staff that gave them significant cause for concern. Their worries were so serious that they kept particular pupils away from Leat because his interest in them appeared to be highly suspicious. Yet of these 30 incidents, only 11 were reported by staff. And when they did report their concerns, Leat was only 'spoken to' by the head teacher. This potential inertia is a serious issue for you as a safeguarding lead and you must ensure that your whistleblowing policies and procedures are the subject of regular staff training. This will reinforce the duty of staff to report their suspicions and to make sure they're aware of the protections available to them if they were to whistleblow themselves.[19]

Managing 'low-level' concerns about adults

When an allegation of abuse about an adult in a school or college is made, there's clear guidance about how you should handle it. But what about concerns that fall below that threshold? It's important that any concerns about an adult working or volunteering in your setting are reported at an early stage, and that everyone in the organisation has confidence in the system. This is part of building a strong safeguarding culture.

It is important for you to have a mechanism for the reporting of 'low-level' concerns about adults, together with clear guidance for staff on how to raise any such concerns. In 2020, Farrer & Co LLP, an independent law firm with a specialism in safeguarding, produced a helpful set of guidelines on this subject: *Developing and Implementing a Low-level Concerns Policy: A Guide for Organisations*

---

[19] 'Whistleblowing for employees'. Available from www.gov.uk/whistleblowing [accessed 15 January 2020].

which Work with Children.[20] This sets out what organisations need to consider when developing an approach to managing low-level concerns that fit into this category. Based on research conducted on 20 Serious Case Reviews, the guidance focuses on adult behaviour towards children and encourages organisations to adopt a low-level concern policy that:

o empowers staff to share any low-level concern about an adult with the safeguarding lead;

o ensures that staff are clear about, and confident to distinguish, expected and appropriate behaviour from concerning and problematic or inappropriate behaviour;

o addresses unprofessional behaviour and helps the individual to correct such behaviour at an early stage;

o provides a responsive, sensitive and proportionate handling of such concerns when they are raised; and

o helps to identify any weaknesses in the organisation's safeguarding system.

There's strong evidence that in cases where systematic abuse has been perpetrated by an adult in an organisation, including schools, other members of staff were often already concerned about the person's behaviour. It's vital that staff have the confidence to report any concerns, and that those concerns are properly recorded so any potential patterns of behaviour can be identified as early as possible.

Record keeping

KCSIE clearly states that if you find an allegation against a member of staff to be false or malicious, you need to remove it from their personnel record. However, for all other allegations,

---

[20] Farrer & Co, *Developing and Implementing a Low-level Concerns Policy: A Guide for Organisations which Work with Children*, 2020. Available from www. farrer.co.uk/globalassets/clients-and-sectors/safeguarding/low-level-concerns-guidance-2020.pdf [accessed 1 January 2021].

it's important to record a clear and comprehensive summary of the allegation, and details of how it was followed up and resolved, any action you took and what decisions you made. You also need to give a copy to the person concerned.

The purpose of this record is to be able to give accurate information if the staff member asks for a reference in future. It will also give clarification in situations in which future Disclosure and Barring Service (DBS) checks reveal information from the police about an allegation that didn't result in a criminal conviction, and it will help to prevent an unnecessary re-investigation if, as sometimes happens, an allegation re-surfaces after a period of time.

You need to be aware that schools and colleges have an obligation to preserve records that contain information about allegations of sexual abuse against staff for the use of the Independent Inquiry into Child Sexual Abuse (there's further information on the IICSA website).[21] Records of all other allegations against staff should be retained until the accused person has reached normal pension age, or for ten years from the date of the allegation if that's longer.

Key learning points

- How you manage concerns can have a significant impact on the protection afforded to a child or the outcome of legal proceedings, which may be some years hence; you need to begin with the end in mind.
- It is essential that all staff understand the thresholds for recording concerns and the importance of recording the right information in the right way.
- The type of system in which you record your information can make or break your case

---

[21] Independent Inquiry into Child Sexual Abuse. Available from www.iicsa.org.uk [accessed 17 December 2020].

management process – technology can have a huge part to play in improving the effectiveness of your safeguarding practice.

- You and your staff need to know how to react and respond to sensitive disclosures from pupils.
- It's important that you and other relevant staff members know how to respond to serious or complex incidents and allegations against adults.
- Your policies and procedures for whistleblowing should form part of staff safeguarding training.

Chapter 4
Your external network
Working with others

As you'll have gathered by now, a key part of your role is to collaborate with people inside your own organisation. However, it doesn't stop there. Just as important is how well you work with external agencies such as the police, children's social care, healthcare professionals and other external partners – whether they be agencies or individual people.

To understand the necessity and complexity of multi-agency working, we need to go back to 1973. This was the year that Maria Colwell, a seven-year-old girl from Brighton, was killed by her stepfather, and it's a case that became a turning point in the development of UK safeguarding practice. It's worth reminding ourselves of the details of that case as a way of getting under the skin of what it means to work effectively across agencies, because it led to the first of the multi-agency arrangements that we see formalised today.

Investigations showed that, two years prior to her death, Maria had become increasingly distressed during visits to her future stepfather, William Kepple. Neighbours frequently reported signs of her abuse and neglect to both the NSPCC and the Housing Department, but those concerns don't appear to have been taken seriously and during the second half of 1972 Maria wasn't seen at all by her social worker, who wrongly thought the NSPCC was visiting her. In the final few months of her life, Maria stopped attending school but despite neighbours and teachers reporting further concerns about her welfare to various agencies (she was 'almost a walking skeleton'), she was allowed to remain with her family. One night, when Maria's mother had kept her up late to act as a buffer against her violent husband, Kepple repeatedly kicked Maria and she died the following day. Kepple was initially convicted of her murder, but this was reduced to manslaughter on appeal and his initial sentence halved to just four years after he cited diminished responsibility due to his being drunk at the time.

In the report following Maria's killing it transpired, among other things, that the family's social worker had returned her to the family home without consulting a psychiatrist or paediatrician; that her supervision order had been split between Brighton and East Sussex councils, which meant her social worker wasn't privy to all the information she needed; that there was no communication between police and social services about the neighbours' concerns; that neither the education welfare officer nor the health visitor knew that Maria was under supervision; and that although the infant school staff knew about the supervision, there was nothing in her records about this. The school record cards held inadequate information and were not seen as important by teachers, and the slips passed between teachers and education welfare officers were insufficient as a record-keeping device. This meant that when she moved from infant to junior school, the staff were unaware of her situation and therefore didn't send essential information to Maria's social worker.

The overall conclusion was that communication and co-ordination within and between agencies had been (in the dry language of report writing) 'unsatisfactory'. East Sussex County Council was held to be primarily responsible for the failures that led to Maria's death, but the report stated that Brighton Council and the NSPCC had also failed her and that the police should have passed on what little information they had. There were conflicts of evidence between the schools and social services, partly because teachers had recorded very little and the note-keeping by social workers was 'variable'.

Maria's case captured public attention and the media called for action, leading to the establishment of what we think of as modern child protection practices. The poor communication between statutory agencies resulted in the introduction of Area Child Protection Committees (ACPCs) in England and Wales, and also the emergence of child protection conferences, which assessed individual cases in a cross-agency way. The 'At Risk Register' in each local area was also born. Several more high-profile child death scandals, including those of Jasmine Beckford, Toni-Ann Byfield, and Victoria Climbié, all beyond tragic, eventually resulted in the 2002 green paper known as *Every Child Matters*[1] and the Children Act 2004. The Children Act also introduced Serious Case Reviews (SCRs) to look into cases in which a child had died or come to serious harm as a result of abuse or neglect. The purpose of SCRs was to create learning opportunities for agencies and professionals, so they could improve the way they worked together to safeguard children. A Local Safeguarding Children Board (LSCB) – the successor body to ACPCs – was able to commission a review for a case from which it was believed something could be learned to improve local practice. Despite all this, it was over 30 years from the time of Maria Colwell's killing before agencies were required by law to ensure the free flow of information about child protection and safeguarding.

---

[1] HM Treasury, *Every Child Matters*, September 2003. Available from www.gov.uk/government/publications/every-child-matters [accessed 17 December 2020].

What can we take from this when we consider how schools work with external agencies? For a start, the failure of different organisations to work effectively with one another is a key theme in many case reviews; this goes for schools liaising with agencies, as well as agencies communicating with schools and with each other. Secondly, it's clear that working across agencies is one of the most challenging activities in safeguarding. So challenging, in fact, that time after time the lessons identified in the litany of tragedies don't appear to have been learned.

Why do we keep getting it wrong? It's clear that working with others is necessary but for some reason it is intractably difficult, yet does it have to be? Our aim in this chapter is to help you to understand the barriers to working effectively with external agencies and to give you strategies for overcoming some of the problems you might encounter. When you consider that the number of referrals from schools to children's social care alone is about 117,000 a year (about 18% of the national total), you can see why finding ways to work effectively with those outside your school is so important.[2]

Multi-agency working – the context

Safeguarding is very much about teamwork, and collaboration is at the heart of effective safeguarding practice. It wasn't so long ago that, in many organisations, the safeguarding lead would be reluctant to share information for vaguely expressed 'confidentiality reasons'. These 'reasons' put the interests of data protection above those of child protection, often based on an over-developed sense of risk aversion or a misunderstanding of

---

[2] Department for Education, 'Characteristics of children in need: 2019 to 2020', 26 November 2020. Available from https://explore-education-statistics.service.gov.uk/find-statistics/characteristics-of-children-in-need/2020 [accessed 5 January 2021].

the principles of legality, proportionality, and necessity.[3] However, the current KCSIE guidance (more of which you'll learn about in the next chapter) makes it clear that 'schools and colleges have a pivotal role to play in multi-agency safeguarding arrangements',[4] and encourages safeguarding leads and practitioners to share information with whomever they need to, providing it can be justified. The aim of all agencies should be to build up a shared picture about the risk surrounding a particular child, and to do that they each need to know what's going on. One of the outcomes of this shift in thinking has been some fundamental structural changes in the way that agencies are now expected to work together. This gives you a more solid framework to operate within than you have ever had before.

However, despite these developments, in recent years there have continued to be a number of high-profile cases in which children have been killed or seriously harmed, and in many of them a lack of information sharing has been identified as a major contributory or causal factor. In 2006, the UK government introduced a key piece of statutory guidance called *Working Together to Safeguard Children*, which set out the ways in which a wide range of organisations, agencies, and individuals (including public, private, and third sector bodies) should work together to safeguard and promote the wellbeing of children.[5] This guidance

---

[3] The 1988 Crime and Disorder Act first put information sharing between agencies on a statutory footing for the purpose of preventing crime and disorder. The Data Protection Act 1998 (now superseded by the Data Protection Act 2018 and the General Data Protection Regulation – GDPR) and the Human Rights Act 1998 later added further rigour to the legal framework.

[4] KCSIE 2020, Paragraph 74.

[5] *Working Together to Safeguard Children* has been regularly updated since 2006 and the latest version was published in September 2018. Available from https://assets.publishing.service.gov.uk/government/uploads/system/uploads/attachment_data/file/779401/Working_Together_to_Safeguard-Children.pdf [accessed 17 December 2020].

forms the basis for all multi-agency working and safeguarding practice, including:

o the assessment of need and early help;
o organisational responsibilities;
o multi-agency safeguarding arrangements;
o improving child protection and safeguarding practice; and
o child death reviews.

In 2014, the Home Office produced a report on multi-agency working called the *Multi-Agency Working and Information Sharing Project*, which led to the adoption of Multi-Agency Safeguarding Hubs (MASH) in local authority areas.[6] The role of a MASH is to bring the relevant statutory agencies together in one physical or virtual place, so they can work closely together to safeguard children and vulnerable adults in their locality. The hubs are based on three common principles:

o effective information sharing between agencies;
o joint risk assessment and decision-making; and
o co-ordinated response and intervention.

The introduction of a MASH in many local authority areas has undoubtedly led to improvements in safeguarding practice, especially when assessing risk and need. Having access to a wider range of information from the different agencies has helped to build a more complete picture of risk.

The Wood Review

A further development in this area was the publication in 2016 of *The Wood Review*, which identified that LSCBs in England weren't

---

[6] Home Office, *Multi-Agency Working and Information Sharing Project: Final Report*, July 2014. Available from https://assets.publishing.service.gov.uk/government/uploads/system/uploads/attachment_data/file/338875/MASH.pdf [accessed 17 December 2020].

fit for purpose and recommended their reform.[7] In 2019, new local safeguarding partnership arrangements were introduced, which brought together the police, the local authority, and the local clinical commissioning groups (known as the three 'safeguarding partners'). The significance of this shift is in how it has streamlined the approach to multi-agency working. In our past lives as police officers, we regularly sat on LSCBs and were faced with 20 people around a table who didn't always understand their roles. As a result, it was often difficult to get things done. The new system promises to be less bureaucratic, with fewer agencies at the 'top table', although a key test of its effectiveness will be how the three partners interact with each other and collaborate with other agencies, including nurseries, schools, and colleges.

From your perspective, the way you access support and advice from local agencies hasn't changed as a result of the new three-agency framework. This is a strategic-level change rather than an operational one, so on a day-to-day basis you can still talk to the same people in the same organisations as you always have done. KCSIE 2020 states that the Designated Safeguarding Lead is expected to act as a point of contact with the three safeguarding partners, but whether that's purely a tactical role, or one that will give you the opportunity to influence safeguarding strategy, has yet to be seen.

The Wood Review also led to the reform of Serious Case Reviews (SCRs) in England, which had been criticised for their lack of independence, with agencies effectively 'marking their own homework'. SCRs were intended to be for the purpose of learning, not for apportioning blame. There was also frustration about the time SCRs took to complete (often many years) and the

---

[7] Department for Education, *Wood Report: Review of the Role and Functions of Local Safeguarding Children Boards*, March 2016. Available from https://assets.publishing.service.gov.uk/government/uploads/system/uploads/attachment_data/file/526329/Alan_Wood_review.pdf [accessed 17 December 2020].

lack of transparency for the families of the victims. In 2019, SCRs were replaced in England by Child Safeguarding Practice Reviews (CSPRs), overseen by a national Child Safeguarding Practice Review Panel. The purpose of a CSPR is to 'focus on improving learning, professional practice and outcomes for children', although it's not yet clear whether they will be any quicker, more transparent, or more effective than SCRs.[8]

Wales Safeguarding Procedures

The *Wales Safeguarding Procedures*, launched in December 2019, provide an overarching legal framework for every agency in Wales with a responsibility for safeguarding children and adults at risk.[9] The procedures set out principles and clear 'pointers for practice' across a wide range of safeguarding topics, all designed to support practitioners, and outline the framework for determining how individual child protection referrals, actions, and plans are managed. Partnership working and communication between agencies is seen as crucial in identifying vulnerable children and helping to keep them safe from harm. A key piece of statutory guidance, *Working Together to Safeguard People*,[10] underpins these all-Wales procedures and emphasises the need for agencies to work closely together to protect children, and details the procedures statutory agencies should follow. In addition, there's

---

[8] Child Safeguarding Practice Review Panel, 'About us'. Available from www.gov.uk/government/organisations/child-safeguarding-practice-review-panel/about [accessed 17 December 2020]. Similar reviews in other parts of the UK are known as Child Practice Reviews (Wales), Significant Case Reviews (Scotland) and Case Management Reviews (Northern Ireland).

[9] *Wales Safeguarding Procedures*, 2019. Available from https://safeguarding.wales [accessed 17 December 2020].

[10] Welsh Government, *Working Together to Safeguard People*, last updated November 2019. Available from https://gov.wales/safeguarding-people-introduction [accessed 17 December 2020].

specific guidance for education, *Keeping Learners Safe* (2020),[11] which sets out the role of local authorities, governing bodies, and proprietors of independent schools. This document also gives detailed advice for safeguarding leads about handling concerns in schools.

The key message to take from the English and Welsh guidance is that information sharing has a critical role to play in effective safeguarding. While data protection legislation gives necessary protections for citizens and provides frameworks for professional practice, it shouldn't prevent you from sharing information when you need to for safeguarding purposes.

Multi-agency working – why is it so hard?

Our previous experience has shown us that multi-agency working isn't for the faint-hearted, and there are some understandable reasons for this. Despite all the improvements that have been made to child protection and safeguarding processes, there are still fundamental challenges within them that make them susceptible to failure – the most obvious being the difficulties inherent in agencies working together. Of course, no one goes into safeguarding to fail, and most of the people we've met during both our policing careers and in our current roles are incredibly professional and committed to protecting children and young people, and they do it well. So why is it so hard for them to succeed at times? Let's look at where the problems lie.

Different agencies have their own priorities and cultures

An organisation's culture is made up of myriad assumptions, habits, and beliefs, which are rarely acknowledged but play a fundamental part in how people think, feel, and express

---

[11] Welsh Government, *Keeping Learners Safe*, October 2020. Available from https://gov.wales/keeping-learners-safe [accessed 17 December 2020].

themselves. As a result, organisations can have a range of approaches to safeguarding because they're looking at the same problem but from very different perspectives.

In a complex case, multiply these different cultures by three or four agencies and it's not hard to see how misunderstandings and even conflicts can arise.

Different agencies have their own systems and processes

Every agency has its own systems, processes, and procedures, which have developed over time and are exclusive to it. What's more, the system for managing safeguarding data within each is likely to vary and is not usually accessible to anyone outside of the organisation. This means that an individual agency can access its own information about a child or family, but will rarely have the complete picture. The result of this is that it can be difficult for people to understand the relevance of a piece of information when they don't have access to other key facts.

Practical communication difficulties

When busy diaries make even day-to-day communication between colleagues *within* agencies difficult, it's not hard to see how maintaining regular and meaningful communication *between* organisations is always going to be challenging. For safeguarding leads in schools, it can be particularly difficult once the school day has begun, and in agencies such as the police you'll find that staff work variable shift patterns, which may make them unavailable when you need to speak to them.

Levels of knowledge and training vary across agencies

The content and quality of training can vary greatly between agencies, and this lack of consistency means that staff in different organisations aren't always on the same page in terms of their knowledge and understanding. Each agency commissions or delivers its own safeguarding training and standards can differ from area to area. A rare but notable exception to this is the Joint Interview Training in England and Wales, which was developed by the police service, the Crown Prosecution Service, the Department for Education, the Department for Health, and the Welsh Assembly Government.[12]

Resources are stretched across the board

Most public sector organisations have seen significant budget cuts in recent years, and these have had an impact on staffing levels. When demand is high, tensions can arise between agencies, especially when people feel frustrated about not having the time to do safeguarding well. One of the major issues raised by safeguarding leads in schools is the lack of capacity within other agencies to take on new cases. While the number of cases meeting the local authority threshold is high, there's increasing concern that referrals from schools aren't being accepted due to reduced staffing in children's social care. This means that schools are often managing challenging safeguarding cases without the support of other agencies, and with stretched resources themselves.

The complexities of information sharing

As you can see, even when things go well, there are barriers to effective multi-agency working. For instance, some safeguarding leads in MATs can be dealing with any number of different local authorities across England. One such person who we

---

[12] Ministry of Justice, *Achieving Best Evidence in Criminal Proceedings: Guidance on Interviewing Victims and Witnesses, and Guidance on Using Special Measures*, March 2011. Available from www.cps.gov.uk/sites/default/files/documents/legal_guidance/best_evidence_in_criminal_proceedings.pdf [accessed 17 December 2020].

spoke to recently explained that she was liaising with 23 local authorities. Each had different referral forms for her to complete, different thresholds for referral, and different approaches to case conferencing, case management, and safeguarding training. This inconsistency has a direct impact on the children in the schools across her MAT because they were receiving variable levels of support.

The requirements of multi-agency working and the complexity of the issues related to information sharing, particularly with local authorities, is a significant call on the time and skills of busy safeguarding leads in schools and colleges. Safeguarding leads consistently report that this is one of their biggest challenges, and they often complain that while local authorities and other agencies are constantly seeking information from them, those agencies are often reticent to reciprocate, even when it would seem essential for the school or college to be told for a very clear safeguarding purpose. This perceived resistance of local authorities and other agencies to sharing information with schools and colleges while constantly demanding information from them can lead to tensions in the relationships between safeguarding leads and their local authority partners. If all agencies are to be truly focused on the safeguarding and wellbeing of children, the information flow needs to work in both directions so that all of the relevant agencies and organisations, including schools and colleges, can be more aware of the potential risks and vulnerabilities.

Getting onto the same page

Let's start with your relationships with external agencies – how would you rate the effectiveness of your current relationship with children's social care, your LADO, and the police? The better you know each other, the more able you'll be to deal with any communication problems when they arise, and that means getting to know them in a proactive way. For example, you can help them to understand your role and the types of safeguarding cases you're managing, as well as any concerns you might have about multi-agency working. Not only will this make your safeguarding more effective, but you'll also understand their priorities and the challenges they are facing.

We have extensive personal experience of multi-agency working in safeguarding cases, at major incidents and during criminal investigations, and believe us when we say there is no better feeling than seeing a friendly face or hearing a well-known voice when you need help. Joint training and exercises to test multi-agency plans are great opportunities for forging these relationships – not in the midst of a critical incident! If you are a new safeguarding lead (or deputy), do go out of your way to introduce yourself and get to know your multi-agency colleagues (this requires you to find out who they are and how to contact them, which is a perfect start!).

Also, don't undervalue the power of the informal phone call. Often the best way to get an independent view about a concern you may have for a child is simply to pick up the phone to your local children's social care team and ask for advice. There's no need to wait until you have to make it formal, at which point the whole process can feel quite daunting. Of course, this is a lot easier if you have a pre-existing relationship with some of the people there, and an understanding of how they work. Having someone at the other end of the phone whom you know is willing to talk to you because you've built up a level of trust and understanding can save you an awful lot of time and stress. Encouragingly, some social care departments now operate a professional consultation line for this purpose, which offers either phone or web chat options.

Another way you can help yourself is to know what kind of information external agencies are looking for and how to communicate it. It's important that you have a good understanding of the referral process in your area and other agencies' expectations of you. Recently, I was talking with a social worker who told me that the content of many of the school assessments she reads doesn't cover some of the basic details she would expect; she therefore finds it hard to decide if it's reached the local authority threshold. Different agencies have different ways of describing the same event and they use their own terminology, so if you don't 'tick the right box' with your language and communicate things in a way that the recipient wants to receive it, you might have a problem. It comes down to understanding other people and what they want.

A word of caution with this. We regularly speak with safeguarding leads who, on making a referral to children's social care, are asked by social workers to put additional questions to children to glean further information and, in some cases, to speak to siblings or other children to corroborate what's been said. While KCSIE states that 'staff should expect to support social workers and other agencies following any referral', you have to be careful that what you're asked to do doesn't amount to an 'investigation'; that's the responsibility of another agency and for which you have no training, expertise, experience or authority.[13] Apart from anything else, any inappropriate action on your part could jeopardise subsequent legal proceedings, so if you feel that what you're being asked to do is not within your remit you should say so. Many local authority areas have protocols between agencies that allow such decisions to be escalated to a higher level if there's a disagreement between the parties. If you feel you're being asked to go beyond your remit, you should insist on using those provisions; it's only fair to the child, to the case, and to you.

Working with specialist services

Today, safeguarding leads are having increasing contact with specialist services such as mental health teams. The crisis in

---

[13] KCSIE 2020, Paragraph 9, p. 6.

children's and young people's mental health is real and urgent, and it's estimated that over a million young people in the UK have a diagnosable mental health problem.[14] In 2018, the Department of Education published advice to schools in England: *Mental Health and Behaviour in Schools*.[15] Much of the guidance focuses on how you should handle mental health issues with other members of staff, but it also explains that schools should have clear systems and processes for referring children to the healthcare system, including CAMHS and CYPMHS.[16] It also says it's important for schools to understand what local services are available, and how and when to commission them.

One of the most significant updates in KCSIE 2020 is an increased focus on mental health, which emphasises that 'only appropriate trained professionals should attempt to make a diagnosis of a mental health problem'.[17] Governing bodies and proprietors are required to have clear systems and processes for identifying mental health problems, routes to escalation, and referral and accountability systems. The Department for Education, supported by NHS England, has commissioned the Anna Freud Centre to deliver the Link Programme, which will bring together education and mental health services so that children and young people can get the help they need, when they need it. Co-ordinated by local clinical commissioning groups (CCGs), it will be rolled out to all schools and colleges in England over the next four years.[18]

---

[14] YoungMinds, *Impact Report 2018–2019*. Available from https:// youngminds.org.uk/media/3396/impact-report-2018-19-low-res.pdf [accessed 17 December 2020].

[15] Department for Education, *Mental Health and Behaviour in Schools*, November 2018. Available from www.gov.uk/government/publications/ mental-health-and-behaviour-in-schools--2 [accessed 17 December 2020].

[16] CAMHS: Child and Adolescent Mental Health Services; CYPMHS: Children and Young People's Mental Health Services.

[17] KCSIE 2020, Paragraph 35.

[18] Anna Freud National Centre for Children and Families, 'The Link Programme'. Available from www.annafreud.org/schools-and-colleges/

In England, you also need to be aware of the guidance relating to Education, Health and Care plans (usually referred to as EHCPs or EHCs), which in 2014 replaced 'statements' for children with special educational needs and disabilities.[19] You and your school have a pivotal role to play in relation to EHCPs, and it's important that you understand these responsibilities.

Working with the courts and the legal system

If you're the safeguarding lead in a serious case, it's likely that you'll come into contact with the legal profession. You'll certainly be expected to attend case conferences with other statutory agencies, and if legal proceedings are underway you may be asked to meet with legal representatives, or even to give evidence in court. If this happens, it's important that you're prepared for what might lie ahead. The best way to illustrate this is through the experience of a safeguarding lead in England who was asked to give evidence in the Family Court. After the event, a colleague of hers could see how distressed she was, even to the point of being on the verge of resigning, so she asked me to call the safeguarding lead to debrief what had happened. Here's what the safeguarding lead told me.

Risks to a family of children at the school had been identified, and five referrals about them had been made to children's social care. The case ended up at a Family Court hearing, and the safeguarding lead was called to give evidence. Having never done this before, she assumed that all she had to do was to tell the truth and explain what she had done and why. She was nervous, as anyone would be, but didn't expect any major problems. However, when she

---

research-and-practice/the-link-programme [accessed 17 December 2020].

[19] Gov.uk, 'Children with special educational needs and disabilities (SEND)'. Available from www.gov.uk/children-with-special-educational-needs/extra-SEN-help [accessed 17 December 2020].

arrived at court she immediately saw that she was the only party without legal representation; the parents, the local authority, and social care all had lawyers by their sides. This was worrying.

When she was called to the witness box (and it is often a raised wooden 'box', enclosed on three sides with steps up it, like a small church pulpit!), she felt completely alone, and was unprepared for the hostile cross-examination she faced. Question after question was flung her way, and she was interrogated on her safeguarding procedures and processes as well as on her record keeping and the actions that she and other staff had taken. She barely had time to think before the next challenge came. Her description of the experience was that it was 'intimidating', and that she felt as if she was the one on trial. She felt destroyed.

Unfortunately, in our experience of having attended court on countless occasions as police officers, this is not particularly unusual. It's natural to assume you don't need legal representation just to give evidence as a witness, but imagine this. You are asked to take a religious oath (or swear an affirmation) and introduced to the court as the safeguarding lead for your setting. Whether you've got five minutes' or 15 years' experience of the role, you're expected to know your procedures inside out. Lawyers love to challenge witnesses on procedure because it's an easy way to discredit their evidence; if the magistrate or jury start doubting a witness's professional knowledge or abilities, whatever else they say about the case becomes suspect. Of course, for you it's unrealistic to hold all your policies in your head, so if you're likely to become involved in legal proceedings or to have to go to court, our strong recommendation is to seek legal advice and push the local authority, your school or your multi-academy trust to support you in accessing it (it costs money, which is why you might receive some pushback). You should never appear in court to give evidence unless you have had someone to advise you on what you need to prepare for on the day. It's a frightening experience to be exposed in the same way this teacher was.

So what happened with her? In her case, her head teacher had written a letter to the court to say he had delegated the responsibility for safeguarding to her, and this was read out to the court. In other words, he had simply washed his hands of the situation. You can imagine how she felt. At the end of our phone call, trying to cheer her up, I jokingly suggested she take the rest of the afternoon off and play some golf (it was a Friday afternoon in term time). To which she replied that her head teacher was already on the course and had left her in charge – another shining example of his ability to 'delegate'.

Working with parents

Parents and people with parental rights have legal responsibility for their children and they are key stakeholders in the safeguarding process, so it's important to communicate with them well. They should understand how you manage safeguarding so that, should they have a concern about a child (including their own), they know how to report it to you. It's important that they feel confident in your ability to manage difficult situations such as accusations of bullying and mental health concerns, as well as more serious and complex issues which may involve the police and other agencies.

You don't need us to tell you that managing safeguarding concerns with parents can be incredibly challenging (and there appears to be a dearth of training about managing such cases). On occasion you might have to withhold information from parents because you're concerned about compromising an investigation; for instance, if a child's disclosure implicates their parent. Also, you may often find yourself having to advise parents on their own behaviour and signposting them to support, something we frequently hear about safeguarding leads having to do. In addition, you'll find yourself having to explain the rationale for your decisions, which they might not agree with. This is another reason it's important to record not only your decisions but the reasons for them.

The kind of relationship you have with parents largely depends on the level of trust they have in you and your school. Developing an open and transparent approach, in which parents feel engaged and believe that their children are safe, is critical. Parents can have a significant part to play in supporting your safeguarding policies; as adults they also have a safeguarding responsibility and can play an important role in keeping children safe. That said, there will be times when parents or caregivers are the source of the harm a child is enduring, so this is another area in which you need to be relentlessly vigilant.

Your governing body

It's worth remembering that your governing body or board of trustees can influence how your school interacts with other agencies. Governors and trustees should understand the importance of multi-agency working and how it contributes to effective safeguarding. From a strategic perspective, they need to know the arrangements for joint working in your area and how well it operates, so that when you're concerned about external agencies you have their help in challenging decisions. This will support you in your role.

Of all the agencies we've mentioned, it's schools that are usually best placed to identify the signs and symptoms of safeguarding issues at an early stage. That's because they're the ones with the most day-to-day contact with children and their families. Another reason is that in most schools there's a high level of trust between staff, children, and parents, which encourages children to see school and college staff as people who will take their concerns seriously.

As you can see, your school's relationship with other agencies is vital in building up a picture around a child and their family, so that you can identify any risks. This is what makes developing excellent relationships with these organisations so important:

they're the channel through which you help children. If the agencies can understand your context and you can appreciate theirs, you'll find it easier to communicate some of the many complex and difficult issues you deal with. It will give you a head start. If they don't know where you're coming from, and don't understand the risks you're trying to manage in your school, life can only be more difficult.

Key learning points

- Lack of effective communication and information sharing between agencies is routinely the single most important factor highlighted in case reviews.
- Working across agencies is one of the most challenging aspects of safeguarding, not least because of the varying objectives, cultures, and systems within each agency.
- Be proactive; excellent communication and relationship building is the key to improving multi-agency working. The best time to build relationships is rarely in the middle of a crisis.
- Appropriate data sharing reduces risk and makes multi-agency working far more effective (it also saves time and money!).
- Parents and caregivers are a major part of the safeguarding picture and it's important to communicate with them well.

Chapter 5
Child protection and data protection

Information management

In the 1980s, I was a detective sergeant working in inner London. House burglaries and car crime were running at record levels, the majority of which were committed by juvenile offenders.[1] As a supervisor in a specialist burglary investigation team, I was often in charge of officers who were sent out on early morning operations to arrest suspects on the basis of forensic evidence from crime scenes.

One particular morning stands out as a day I'll never forget. I set off to make an arrest at a flat in one of the Peabody estates that house so many people in London. The lad I intended to arrest was 14 years old, and his fingerprints had been identified at the scene of a break-in that had occurred at a house in the same borough several weeks previously. The

---

[1] Young offenders aged 10 to 17 are classed as juvenile offenders. Between the ages of 18 and 21 they're classed as young offenders, while offenders aged 21 and over are known as adult offenders.

property that had been stolen in the burglary was probably long gone, and given his age and family circumstances this was to be a knock on the door (not what the media likes to call a 'dawn raid').

I gave the door a firm rap and waited – the occupants were probably still in bed. Despite hearing movement within the flat the door remained unanswered, so I knocked again and announced loudly that it was the police. After more shuffling noises, the door was opened by a woman with deep bags under her red-rimmed eyes. I asked for her son by name, and her face crumpled. A moment later her expression changed to one of anger as she shouted the words, 'he's dead!' The look of shock on my face must have been obvious because she immediately clarified, 'he's been murdered.' I was rocked beyond words and couldn't believe the distress that I'd just inflicted on this poor woman. Her son had just been killed, and one of her first visitors was a police officer who'd come to arrest him. Stammering my profuse apologies, I left, but I knew I could never undo the harm that I'd caused.

One of the actions we always took before going out to make any arrest was to check police records to ensure the person wasn't already in police custody or in prison, or that they weren't wanted for another offence by other officers. As usual I'd made those checks before going out that morning, but none of our systems had told me that the boy had been murdered by a paedophile in another police force area. That information just hadn't reached our systems. It should have done.

***

This story illustrates the critical role of information sharing. We've already talked about record keeping, but what we haven't considered is the topic of information management as a whole, and how important it is in developing your safeguarding practice. Information management is the process of collecting, storing, managing, and maintaining information in all its forms. It's a broad term, and includes all the policies and procedures you need to have in place for this, as well as enabling you to share appropriate information with different people, organisations, and systems. With the increasing amount of data your school or college now has to manage, a key part of your role is not only how it's looked after but also whether you're putting it to the right use.

Broadly speaking, there are four aspects to information management in safeguarding.

1. The legal considerations (which encompass data protection laws and guidance).
2. Information security (human, physical, and technical).
3. Information sharing.
4. The strategic management of information (how you can use data for planning and to enable action to be taken).

Understanding the legislation and guidance is an essential start, because once you know what you're allowed (and not allowed) to do you'll feel more confident about handling and sharing data. You also need to know what you're doing because of the damaging impact that poor information management can have on people, and the serious financial and legal ramifications for your organisation. But the concept of information management is much wider than just compliance with the law. It's also about how you can treat information as a strategic asset that can give you meaningful insights and a heightened awareness of safeguarding risks and concerns. And if it's shared in the right way, it can open up opportunities to work collaboratively with other agencies as well as with your own staff.

Taking the legal and security aspects first, we'll explore what you need to know when you're processing and controlling data. We always advise safeguarding leads to imagine having to justify any of their decisions in court; in this chapter, we'll take you through the legal and security aspects of information management, so your approach is as watertight as possible. We'll also debunk some myths and explain the principles to work by so you know what you're doing.

With the information sharing and strategic aspect of information management, the sky's the limit as to what you can achieve.

Thinking strategically about it encourages you to ask yourself what you want to achieve with the information you hold. If one of your aims is to increase your safeguarding efficiency, that's one way of thinking about data. If it's to protect children more effectively, that's another way. And if it's to ensure that senior managers, governors, and trustees understand the key indicators for safeguarding, that's yet another way to think about it. This is why you should always maintain good records, so you can use them to improve your working practices.

We have personal experience of this, both from the work we do now with organisations on safeguarding, and from our time in the police service, where much of our effort was focused on information sharing and working out how to use data to achieve our aims more effectively. Hopefully we'll inspire you to feel confident and, dare we suggest it, excited about how you can manage the information you hold, so it transforms the way you safeguard the children in your care.

Data protection and compliance

The legal landscape for data has shifted considerably in recent years with the introduction of two major changes in legislation: the Data Protection Act 2018 (a significant update on the previous 1998 Act), and the introduction in 2018 of the General Data Protection Regulation (GDPR).

Many safeguarding leads feel uncertain about managing information, and yet it's one of the key issues in safeguarding that you must be confident about, because the operational and legal responsibilities are significant. The GDPR and the Data Protection Act 2018 place an extra onus on all organisations to use their data wisely and with restraint.

Let's be clear at the outset that data protection legislation and safeguarding are not in conflict with each other, quite the reverse.

Both the Data Protection Act and the UK GDPR[2] support the appropriate collection and processing of safeguarding information as well as the sharing of it. The law provides a framework for you to do it safely and securely; it certainly does not prevent it or put barriers in the way.

So let's start with some terminology before we come to some of the principles of legal compliance and data protection. It's important to understand the technical terms because you'll come across them in the guidance, and while you don't need to know them all, there are some that it is important to be familiar with.

Data breach: the accidental or deliberate destruction of, loss of, alteration to, disclosure of, or access to personal data.

Data Controller: the organisation that's the legal entity responsible for the data, and that determines the purpose for which, and the way in which, the data is processed. In most cases the Data Controller is the individual school or college, although in a MAT the trust itself has its own data protection responsibilities and may act as the Data Controller for all its schools.

Data Processor: the person or organisation that processes data on behalf of the Data Controller. This could include third-party software providers processing your data on your behalf, including cloud-based systems which store the data off-site.

Data Protection Impact Assessment (DPIA): this is a process that helps to identify and minimise data protection risks. A DPIA must be conducted for any data processing that's likely to result in a high risk to individuals.

---

[2] In January 2021 the UK Government published an amended version of KCSIE that takes account of the change from the EU GDPR to the UK GDPR: www.gov.uk/government/publications/keeping-children-safe-in-education--2 [accessed 18 January 2021]

Data Protection Officer (DPO): a person who works on behalf of your school, college, MAT, or local authority, who is responsible for data protection issues within their organisation.

Data subject: the person about whom you're processing the data, including pupils, parents, and members of staff.

Personal data: any information which on its own, or in conjunction with other information, can identify an individual (the data subject).

Privacy notice: a document used to set out the organisation's policies in plain and simple language, describing how data will be processed. It's good practice for privacy notices to be updated and brought to the attention of data subjects on a regular basis, such as in an annual reminder from schools and colleges to pupils, parents, caregivers, and staff.

Special category data: extremely sensitive information relating to a person's physical or mental health or condition; sex life and sexual orientation; racial or ethnic origin; or biometric data. It's not lawful for special category data to be processed unless some of the specific exemptions are in place that permit its processing for safeguarding purposes. We'll expand on this later.

Subject access request: a request made by a data subject to access any information about them or their child which is held by the school.

The six principles of data protection

The UK Data Protection Act 2018 and GDPR provide a legal framework that allows organisations (including schools) to process personal data. The six principles should lie at the heart of your approach to managing information, as these are the building blocks for good data protection practice. We won't go into too much detail here, but we'll give you enough to understand what the principles are and how they relate to your role as a safeguarding lead.

1. **Lawfulness, fairness, and transparency:** this principle is self-evident. You need to make sure that your organisation's processes for managing personal data are within the law and that you are open and honest with data subjects. To remain transparent, your organisation should set out its approach in its data protection policy and privacy notice.

    The fact that your organisation will be recording safeguarding concerns and processing personal data and special category data concerning the safety and wellbeing of pupils is a necessary and important aspect of keeping children safe. As a safeguarding lead, you should work with your DPO to ensure that the process for managing safeguarding data is clearly communicated in your privacy notices, so pupils and parents understand how it works.

2. **Purpose limitation:** this means that you should only collect personal data for a specific purpose, clearly state what that purpose is, and only collect it for as long as necessary to complete that purpose.

    Given your objective is to protect children and keep them safe, the rationale for collecting personal data and special category data relating to safeguarding concerns is clear. You don't need to justify collecting data on every occasion, but you do need to ensure that the school's rationale is set out in its policies and privacy notice. Also, all staff need to know the threshold for reporting safeguarding concerns, so as to avoid collecting data that falls outside the requirement.

3. **Data minimisation:** you should only process the personal data you need to achieve your purpose, and no more.

    As a safeguarding lead you have an important role to play in making sure that information about safeguarding concerns submitted by members of staff is aligned with the purpose as defined above. It's also good practice to ensure that members of staff are concise when recording concerns, and avoid recording irrelevant or unnecessary information. This is not only good data protection practice; it is also good safeguarding practice. Remember, the law supports this processing by providing you with a framework within which you can collect, store, and share personal data.

4. **Data accuracy:** this is integral to data protection, and the GDPR states that 'every reasonable step must be taken' to erase or rectify data that's inaccurate or incomplete.

   You should ensure that any information on your records is accurate and can be justified by the person who collected it. The data could eventually form part of a legal process, or be subject to review or inspection.

5. **Storage limitation:** you must delete personal data when it is no longer necessary to retain it, and the ongoing retention of data needs to be justified.

   This is an important consideration, and we'll address it in more detail later on. The most important thing to remember is that data can be retained for *any* period, providing it's necessary and proportionate and that you can justify retaining it. Your organisation should have a data retention and destruction policy and as the safeguarding lead you should make yourself aware of it and work with your DPO to ensure safeguarding data is retained and destroyed in accordance with it.

6. **Integrity and confidentiality:** this principle relates to the security of data. The GDPR makes it clear that 'personal data must be processed in a manner that ensures appropriate security including protection against unauthorised or unlawful processing and against accidental loss, destruction or damage, using appropriate technical or organisational measures'.

The security of safeguarding information is of critical importance given the type of personal data you're processing. Your organisation may hold highly sensitive data about the private lives of pupils and their families, some of which would be categorised as 'special category data'. It's therefore essential that your organisation's systems and processes are secure, and that staff understand their responsibilities when they're handling data.

GDPR: the key themes

When the GDPR was introduced in May 2018, everyone thought the world was coming to an end (very similar to the reaction when the advent of the Year 2000 was a 'thing'). But it didn't turn out that way. In fact, the introduction of the legislation was pretty seamless and complemented the existing UK data protection laws as intended.

The GDPR is a legal framework that requires organisations to protect the personal data and privacy of EU citizens for transactions that occur inside the EU. In early 2020 and with Brexit in mind, the EU GDPR was adapted to create the UK GDPR, which came into effect on 31 January 2020.[3] While for schools and colleges the practical effects of the UK GDPR remain much the same as the EU version, there are some significant changes relating to the primacy of domestic law following Brexit. These apply particularly to national security, the intelligence services, and immigration.

The key themes of the GDPR are underpinned by the six principles of data protection, with a strong emphasis on the rights of data subjects. This focus on the rights of individuals has

---

[3] The Data Protection, Privacy and Electronic Communications (Amendments etc) (EU Exit) Regulations 2019. Available from www.legislation.gov.uk/uksi/2019/419/introduction/made [accessed 17 December 2020].

led to a number of changes, which have given data subjects the rights to:

○ be informed about how their personal data is going to be used, such as through a privacy notice;
○ have access to their data via a 'subject access request';
○ request a modification of their data in order to correct it;
○ 'be forgotten' (or to have their data erased);
○ expect confidentiality and security in the way their data is held; and
○ know how their data is collected, stored, shared, and archived or deleted.

It's important to note that children have the same rights as adults over their personal data.[4] These are set out in Chapters III and VIII of the GDPR, but for ease we've laid them out here. However, please bear in mind that there are certain caveats which relate to children, so we suggest you follow the more detailed guidance on the ICO website.[5]

All data subjects, including children, have the right to:

○ be provided with a transparent and clear privacy notice which explains how their data will be processed;
○ be given a copy of their personal data;
○ have inaccurate personal data rectified and incomplete data completed;
○ exercise the right to be forgotten and have their personal data erased;

---

[4] ICO, 'What rights do children have?' Available from https://ico.org.uk/for-organisations/guide-to-data-protection/guide-to-the-general-data-protection-regulation-gdpr/children-and-the-gdpr/what-rights-do-children-have [accessed 17 December 2020].

[5] ICO, 'Children and the UK GDPR'. Available from https://ico.org.uk/for-organisations/guide-to-data-protection/guide-to-the-general-data-protection-regulation-gdpr/children-and-the-uk-gdpr/ [accessed 3 January 2021].

o restrict the processing in specified circumstances;
o data portability;
o object to processing carried out under the lawful bases of public task or legitimate interests, and for the purposes of direct marketing;
o not be subject to automated individual decision-making, including profiling, which produces legal effects concerning him or her;
o complain to the Information Commissioner's Office (ICO) or another supervisory authority;
o bring legal proceedings against a Data Controller or Processor; and
o claim compensation from a controller or processor for any damage suffered as a result of its non-compliance with the GDPR.

A child can exercise these rights on their own behalf so long as they're competent to do so. In Scotland this normally means a child aged 12 or over, but in the rest of the UK it depends on their level of understanding. A child shouldn't be considered to be competent if they're acting against their own best interests, and a parent can only exercise these rights on behalf of their child if the child gives permission, doesn't have sufficient understanding to do so themselves, or when it's in the best interests of the child.

Your organisation's data protection policy will set out the age (or stage of education) at which a child can exercise their own rights. Most have opted for 13 years old. You should review your data protection policy to ensure you are clear on the approach your organisation takes.

There's also a requirement within the regulations that covers the need for staff training and the appointment of a DPO for each organisation; your setting should have one of these. The role of the DPO is an important one, which is to set standards, create policies, support training, and give advice on data protection matters. You may find that the DPO for your school or college is a shared resource with other settings, and if you are a member of a MAT it could be that the DPO is based centrally. It's a good idea for you to have a strong relationship with your DPO, so you can make sure that proper consideration is given to safeguarding data. It's possible that your DPO might not have any safeguarding experience themselves, so you should be in a good position to advise them on the safeguarding context and how that data is being processed (including the existence of any information-sharing protocols with other agencies).

The Data Protection Act 2018 – special category data

One of the major changes in the 2018 Data Protection Act was the introduction of a number of additional exemptions to the prohibition on the processing of 'special category data', with new definitions of the circumstances under which safeguarding information containing that data can be processed and shared. Due to its sensitive nature, it's unlawful for organisations to process special category data unless there are one or more exemptions in place. For instance, the 2018 Act permits the processing of special category data for safeguarding purposes (under the old Act it related more narrowly to child abuse). Here's the detail for this exemption:

To process special category data you have to be confident that the processing is necessary to protect:

O   a child from neglect or physical, mental, or emotional harm; or
O   the physical, mental, or emotional wellbeing of that child.

You should also be aware that sharing special category data doesn't require the consent of the data subject (or a parent or caregiver) if:

O   a practitioner is unable to obtain consent from the subject; or
O   a practitioner can't be reasonably expected to gain consent; or

o   seeking consent could place a child at risk; and

o   sharing is necessary for reasons of substantial public interest.

The sharing of safeguarding information would inevitably meet the requirements of the necessity test, and in many cases doesn't require consent. On that basis we can assume that the law intends that any material or justifiable step to protect a child at risk can be considered as being of 'substantial public interest', and therefore fulfils the legal requirement.

Many safeguarding leads aren't aware of special category data; when we run seminars and training sessions, we regularly find that safeguarding leads haven't heard of it or don't know enough about it or what it means for them. But the good news is that the new legislation gives you more scope than you previously had to process and share sensitive data when a child is at risk. Essentially, it provides you with a clear legal justification for information sharing for safeguarding purposes.

The transfer, retention, and deletion of data

Safeguarding leads often ask us for advice about data retention and deletion, particularly when they're transferring safeguarding files to other schools or colleges. In many cases, they're confused about the guidance and appear to be receiving conflicting advice from their local authority or other advisors. It's apparent that local authorities across the country have differing policies about this, and the advice they're giving is not always consistent. For instance, when a child transfers to another establishment, some authorities will advise schools to send their safeguarding file to the new setting and to retain a copy of the original. In other areas, the local authority's advice to the originating school or college is that they shouldn't retain *any* safeguarding information.

So what guidance is available and how do you know you're following best practice? One of the most reliable sources of information on this subject is the Information and Records Management Society

(IRMS). The IRMS is a not-for-profit organisation, giving guidance on information management to many different types of settings. They've produced an *Information Toolkit for Schools*,[6] which sets out specific guidelines for the transfer, retention, and deletion of data, including child protection information.[7]

The advice from the IRMS about retention is that schools and colleges should retain child protection data until the person has reached their 25th birthday, and most settings follow this. However, the guidance isn't statutory and there are no legally set time limits. The data protection principles should always apply, so if you have a justification for retaining the data beyond that time limit and it's necessary and proportionate to do so, you can ignore the 25th birthday cut-off date. That's not to say that the IRMS guidance is flawed; in fact, it's sensible advice and in most cases the retention periods are realistic. We're simply pointing out that as the Data Controller you're legally entitled to retain relevant data providing you can justify it.

One of the reasons this is such an important issue is the difficulties experienced in recovering evidence when carrying out non-recent investigations into child sexual abuse. The Independent Inquiry into Child Sexual Abuse (IICSA) has commissioned a number of investigations into historic abuse, and one of the major challenges it's had is the fact that valuable documents and electronic records have been destroyed. On announcing the launch of IICSA, the Home Secretary declared a moratorium on the destruction of relevant material, and in June 2015 the then Chair of the Inquiry wrote to a range of organisations (including all local authorities) setting out what may or may not be destroyed.[8]

---

[6] Information and Records Management Society (IRMS), *Information Toolkit for Schools*, 2019. Available from https://irms.org.uk/general/custom.asp?page=SchoolsToolkit [accessed 17 December 2020].

[7] The IRMS use the term 'child protection' throughout the guidance, which is not defined but is taken to include any data relating to safeguarding.

[8] Independent Inquiry into Child Sexual Abuse, 'Chair of the Inquiry issues guidance on destruction of documents', 23 June 2015. Available from www.

In fact, the IRMS has inserted the requirements in that letter into its own guidance, which is worth reading in full:

> Whilst the Independent Inquiry into Child Sexual Abuse (IICSA) is ongoing, it is an offence to destroy any records relating to the inquiry. It is likely, at the conclusion of the inquiry, that an indication will be given regarding appropriate retention periods for child protection records. More information can be found on the IICSA website. Schools from which a pupil transfers should consider retaining a copy of the child protection file.
>
> Please be aware that under the terms of the Independent Inquiry into Child Sexual Abuse (IICSA) it is an offence to destroy any records that might be of relevance to the Inquiry. This overrides all business, statutory, regulatory or legal retention requirements, including data protection requirements and the data subject's right to erasure. It is anticipated that upon conclusion of the Inquiry, further guidance regarding retention will be published.

This makes it clear that, while IICSA is ongoing, you should retain all child protection data and that to destroy any records is a criminal offence. But how do you decide what information might be of relevance? To answer this, you should understand that IICSA's original moratorium made it clear that the requirement to retain child protection data is broad in scope.[9] It said that organisations should be 'retaining any and all documents (however held) which contain content pertaining directly or indirectly to the sexual abuse of children[10] or to child protection and care'. On that basis, it seems that individual schools should hold on to relevant data, even if they've transferred their child protection files to another school.

---

iicsa.org.uk/news/chair-of-the-inquiry-issues-guidance-on-destruction-of-documents [accessed 17 December 2020].

[9] Independent Inquiry into Child Sexual Abuse, Letter to local authority CEOs. Available from www.iicsa.org.uk/sites/default/files/letter-to-local-authority-ceos.pdf [accessed 17 December 2020].

[10] Any person under 18 years of age.

When it comes to managing the retention of data, it's important to take a balanced approach. The Data Protection Act 2018 adopts the GDPR principle of 'storage limitation', which requires that personal data be kept for no longer than is necessary for the purpose for which the data is being processed. Remember, though, that the legislation doesn't impose specific limits or retention periods. If you can demonstrate through your policies, processes, and working practices that you comply with the 'storage limitation' principle, you're acting in accordance with the law.

Also, bear in mind that your school or college is the Data Controller; in other words, the relevant staff in your setting are the people responsible in law for making decisions about data retention. It's not the place of any other authority or person outside it to order that personal data should either be retained or deleted. That decision should always remain with the Data Controller, and if you can justify it you can (and should) keep it. If another person or organisation tries to direct the action you should take in relation to data retention, ask them to give you the legal basis for their instructions in writing and consider seeking legal advice yourself.

Case study: The Bichard Inquiry

Many of you will recall the terrible case of two 10-year-old girls, Jessica Chapman and Holly Wells, who were murdered by school caretaker Ian Huntley in Soham in August 2002. Following Huntley's conviction, the Home Secretary commissioned a public inquiry to examine concerns about the way critical information about Huntley was managed by the police prior to the murders taking place. The Inquiry was chaired by Sir Michael Bichard and the main purpose was to assess the police intelligence-based record keeping, their vetting practices, and the information sharing with other agencies.

It emerged that Huntley had an extensive record of serious sexual offences against underage girls and young women in the years leading up to the killings. A number of allegations had been made to the police prior to 2002, which indicated that Huntley was a serial offender and a very serious threat to the public, and especially towards young girls. Concerns about Huntley were not adequately investigated. Crucially, records relating to his criminal activity were also destroyed by Humberside Police on the basis that he had not been convicted for these allegations. Humberside Police wrongly believed that under the Data Protection Act it was unlawful to retain any information regarding criminal allegations that had not led to a conviction.

Huntley subsequently applied for a school caretaker's job at Soham Village College in Cambridgeshire under an alias of Ian Nixon. Due to flaws in the school's recruitment processes and in the police vetting procedures, no form of background check was conducted before or after the job interview and Huntley was appointed to this role on a full-time basis despite him having no relevant previous experience. Although Huntley had applied for this job under an alias, his real name appeared on the application form, and had Cambridgeshire Police carried out a check on this name they would have discovered an outstanding burglary charge on file.

The findings of the Bichard Inquiry led directly to the introduction of the Police National Database (PND) to enable the effective sharing of information between police forces; a ground-breaking code of practice on the management of police information (known as MOPI), which introduced strict national standards on police record keeping; and new guidelines on the procedures relating to criminal record checks, which led to the introduction of the Disclosure and Barring Service (DBS) (formerly the Independent Safeguarding Authority).

As an aside, Dorset Police (the force we led at the time) were one of the first forces in the country to fully implement the recommendations from the Inquiry and to introduce a Multi-Agency Information Sharing Protocol to standardise the exchange of information across all of the statutory agencies in the county. In fact, when we launched the protocol Sir Michael Bichard was kind enough to attend the event and featured as our keynote speaker.[11]

Subject access requests

One of the main principles of data protection regulations is that data subjects should be able to access their own data, and the GDPR has strengthened the guidance on this. Before the GDPR was introduced, data subjects were charged a fee for requesting access to their data but this has now been removed; as a result, the number of such requests made to schools, colleges and MATs has increased.

Remember that subject access requests can come from a range of people including pupils, parents, members of staff (including former staff), and volunteers. Data subjects can make a request to:

o confirm whether their personal data is being processed;
o ask the school to provide a copy of their personal data; and
o be informed about the processing of their personal data.

In reality, your DPO will normally take the lead on subject access requests but as a safeguarding lead, you may be asked to help, so here's what you and your DPO need to think about:

o You should take appropriate steps to verify the identity of the person making the request.
o Pupils may raise requests and your establishment needs to comply (either directly to the pupil or to their parent if the pupil is not considered mature enough).
o The response to a request needs to be clear and capable of being understood by the average person (or child).

---

[11] Police Professional, 'A little force goes a long way'. Available from www. policeprofessional.com/news/a-little-force-goes-a-long-way/ [accessed 15 January 2021].

o If the response to a request would disclose the personal data of another person, the request can be refused unless permission has been given by the other data subject.

o Requests need to be completed within one month.

o Relevant staff must be trained to recognise and manage subject access requests.

A major consideration is whether your disclosure of information to a data subject might lead to the risk of harm to any person (especially a child). If there have been allegations of abuse or ill treatment towards a child, you'd need to consider the potential consequences of releasing any information, particularly to a third party. Importantly, there is a legal exemption that your organisation can rely on to withhold personal data from the data subject in these circumstances. This means that safeguarding information does not need to be disclosed if you believe that complying with the right of access would be likely to cause serious harm to the physical or mental health of an individual. In most circumstances, this determination will be made by the safeguarding lead and the DPO jointly.

This is a complex area, especially as there are several other legal provisions in England that relate to parental responsibility and parental access to their child's school records. These differ depending on whether the school is maintained, an academy, or an independent school.[12] The situation can become particularly fraught when the relationships between parents or caregivers break down, such as with divorce, and both parties want access to information about their child – which may or may not relate to safeguarding.[13]

---

[12] The Education (Pupil Information) (England) Regulations 2005. Available from www.legislation.gov.uk/uksi/2005/1437/contents/made [accessed 17 December 2020]; The Education (Independent School Standards) Regulations 2014. Available from www.legislation.gov.uk/uksi/2014/3283/schedule/made [accessed 17 December 2020].

[13] Department for Education, 'Understanding and dealing with issues related to parental responsibility', updated 3 September 2018. Available

There may also be court orders that have to be complied with. It's easy to make a wrong decision in these circumstances, so if you're in any doubt we'd urge you to seek legal advice.

When it comes to disclosing personal data relating to safeguarding to a parent, it is sensible to work with your DPO. We are aware of serious data breaches having taken place in educational settings where safeguarding leads have inadvertently shared information that has caused a great deal of upset to other individuals, at least one of which resulted in the school being sued for damages. We say this not to scare you, but to remind you of the importance of working with your DPO who is trained to support you with such disclosures.

Information sharing and the Seven Golden Rules

In July 2018, the UK government produced a useful, non-statutory advice document called *Information Sharing: Advice for Practitioners*.[14] The aim of this is to support frontline safeguarding practitioners in the decisions they take on information sharing, and the best part is that it's only 16 pages long. If you read only one document on the subject, we recommend that you make it this one, because it embodies a highly practical approach to information sharing that simplifies some of the guidance (without taking any shortcuts).

Contained within the document are what have been called the 'Seven Golden Rules of Information Sharing'. Given how easy

---

from www.gov.uk/government/publications/dealing-with-issues-relating-to-parental-responsibility/understanding-and-dealing-with-issues-relating-to-parental-responsibility [accessed 17 December 2020].

[14] HM Government, *Information Sharing: Advice for Practitioners Providing Safeguarding Services to Children, Young People, Parents and Carers*, July 2018. Available from https://assets.publishing.service.gov.uk/government/uploads/system/uploads/attachment_data/file/721581/Information_sharing_advice_practitioners_safeguarding_services.pdf [accessed 17 December 2020].

it is to feel bogged down by the Data Protection Act 2018 and the GDPR, these rules explain the main principles of information sharing in a way that's easy to understand. Here's our summary of the key points.

1. No barriers to information sharing

Remember that the GDPR, the Data Protection Act 2018, and Human Rights law are not barriers to justified information sharing but provide a clear framework to ensure that personal information about living individuals is shared appropriately. The advice document also states that 'fears about sharing information cannot be allowed to stand in the way of the need to safeguard and promote the welfare of children at risk of abuse and neglect'. As we've seen earlier, the existing legal framework gives sufficient flexibility for you to share information when you need to, providing it's justified.

2. Be open and honest with the subject(s)

It's an important aspect of the GDPR that organisations are open and honest with data subjects (and their families when appropriate) about why, what, how, and with whom information will or could be shared, and seek their agreement unless it's unsafe or inappropriate to do so. This means that your organisation has a duty to ensure the data subject understands what data is held about them and why. This is where your privacy notice comes in.

3. Seek advice from other practitioners

Sometimes information sharing can be complex, and there's no need for you to operate in a bubble. If you're in any doubt about sharing the information concerned, seek advice while avoiding disclosing the identity of the person if you can. In addition to your own DPO, you can also consult your local authority, the ICO, or even take specialist legal advice if you're involved in a complicated situation. The important thing to remember is that there are experts available to help (the ICO is particularly responsive).

4. Where possible, share information with consent

Although you should respect the wishes of those who don't consent to having their information shared, the GDPR and Data Protection Act 2018 empower you to share information without consent if, in your judgement, there's a lawful basis to do so (such as when safety may be at risk). You need to base your judgement on the facts of the case. When you're sharing or requesting personal information from someone, be clear about the basis on which you're doing it. When you don't have consent, be mindful that the person might not expect their information to be shared.

Having said that, we sometimes find that people think they should seek consent when they don't need to. If you know you have a legal justification for sharing and you intend to do so regardless of consent being given, asking for it is meaningless. In these circumstances, you're not carrying out a consultation exercise.

5. Consider safety and wellbeing

Base your information-sharing decisions on considerations of the safety and wellbeing of the individual and any others who may be affected by that individual's actions. This is particularly relevant when handling allegations of abuse between children or against members of staff. For instance, if a serious allegation is made against a child, what information should you share about the alleged perpetrator and with whom, given the information may end up in the public domain? Another example could be when a parent is suspected of physically abusing a child, and it would put the child at greater risk if you told the parent of your concerns.

6. Follow the key principles of sharing information

o Necessary and proportionate: when deciding what information to share, consider how much information you need to release.

o Relevant: only share information that's relevant to the purpose with those who need it.

o Adequate: information should be adequate for its purpose, and of the right quality to ensure that it can be understood and relied upon.

o Accurate: information should be accurate and up to date, and should distinguish between fact and opinion.

o Timely: information should be shared in a timely fashion to reduce the risk of missed opportunities to offer support and protection to a child.

o Secure: whenever possible, information should be shared in an appropriate, secure way. Practitioners must always follow their organisation's policy on data security.

o Record: information-sharing decisions should be recorded, whether or not you decide to share. You need to cite reasons, including what you've shared and with whom.

7. Record your decisions and rationale

Keep a record of your decisions about information sharing and your rationale for them, whether you share information or not. If you decide to share, then record what you've shared, with whom, and for what purpose. If you decide not to share you should record that too, along with the reasons for it.

As chief police officers we were regularly faced with decisions regarding the sharing of incredibly sensitive personal data and special category data. Often that decision was not straightforward and there were many factors to be considered, not least the balancing of our legal responsibilities with the rights of the people whose information was proposed to be shared.

Unless the case is clear cut, it will inevitably be a matter of you and your DPO having to consider the legislation and to use your professional judgement to reach a decision on information sharing; sometimes you may need to seek legal advice, but that should never be an excuse for avoiding or delaying an obvious decision. Whenever we were faced with a finely balanced decision it was always useful to think about who would suffer the most harm if the information was or wasn't shared, although that's not always easy to predict. Ultimately, would you prefer to be held to account for potentially over-sharing information or for failing to prevent serious mental or physical harm to a person? That's not an encouragement to share all information *carte blanche* but in some cases that's the dilemma you may be faced with, so it's as well to discuss with your DPO in advance the framework you would use to make such decisions, and how your decisions and your rationale for those decisions would be recorded. By following the 'Seven Golden Rules' you and your DPO will be in a very strong position to justify your decision-making and to demonstrate the thought processes that led to those decisions.

Developing an information management strategy

One interesting use of safeguarding data that we've come across was at a secondary school in London. The safeguarding lead there had been using our system for three years, so we wanted to catch up with him to discover how he'd been finding it. He told us he'd created a report which showed him that there was a sudden peak in bullying during late October and early November each year. At first, he thought there'd been a mistake, but he re-ran the figures twice more and it was there, clear as day.

So he decided that, given it was September, he'd tackle the problem before it reared its head again. Calling together his team, he drew up a communication plan to highlight what was going on. He even introduced the topic of bullying into assemblies and spoke with pupils to let them know the school knew it was an issue they should be aware of. You could call this the implementation of an intelligent information strategy – one that looks at the data, draws useful conclusions from it, and makes proactive and impactful changes as a result. In this example there was a very significant decrease in bullying which was wholly attributed to the data analysis and the action taken as a consequence.

This shows how, by taking a strategic approach to information management, you can identify underlying trends and be in a good position to anticipate potential vulnerabilities and areas of risk. For instance, setting triggers and alarms by having thresholds in place will tell you whether a certain category of concern has tipped over into being a problem.

Safeguarding leads can sometimes see information management as a bureaucratic process, rather than treating information as a valuable strategic asset that can inform their understanding and drive their safeguarding strategy. However, thinking strategically about it encourages you to ask yourself what you want to achieve with the information you hold. Reliable data should be highlighting trends and informing your priorities, enabling you to communicate clearly to colleagues and other senior leaders, as well as helping you to save time and be efficient. You want to make the most of this asset, so you can identify problems and trends ahead of time which will help you to achieve your main objective – to protect children. It's easy to underestimate how critical your data is to doing that; the key to safeguarding those in your care is under your nose in that filing cabinet or IT system.

Safeguarding always comes down to a combination of people, information and systems, so part of your strategy would be to decide the main formats in which you want to produce your reports. You could see them as a way of running key indicators for your senior leadership or governing body, a chronology review for a case conference, or any other purpose.

Securing safeguarding data

Then there's the 'people' aspect of security, which is probably the most significant risk. You're trusting people with sensitive data, so you need to be clear about what information different members of staff should have access to. What are your policies for this? And how does it work if it's a paper system? Don't forget that your DPO has an important role to play in setting rules around data security.

As we've mentioned, accessibility is a key component of a successful record-keeping arrangement. Many teachers have told us how convenient it is to log onto an online system from home (not least during Covid-19, when they had no alternative), but you also need policies to make sure that when data is accessed remotely it's done in a compliant way. There's also the risk inherent in logging in from a public place. If you're on your phone or using public Wi-Fi, this is clearly not a wise idea, but we come back to the principle of proportionality: if you need urgent access and there's no alternative, the risk may be justified.

If you are using an online recording system for safeguarding these are the kinds of things that are important to agree with users right from the outset.

o   They should use unique passwords and log off each time they finish using the system.
o   They should avoid allowing browsers to remember their usernames and passwords.
o   They are responsible for the security of their passwords and must not allow anyone else to use them.
o   They must immediately change their passwords if these are lost, stolen or otherwise compromised and report what has happened as soon as practicable.
o   They should refer all subject access requests for information from the system to their DPO.
o   They should only use the system in accordance with their organisation's information security policy and the Data Protection Act 2018.
o   If it is necessary to access the system at home, they should use a private space and a secure wireless point, and ensure

that no family member or other person is able to view the system.

o   If they suspect that anyone has gained unauthorised access to the system, they must immediately notify their Data Controller.

And finally, think about the different places in which you store your data. If you use a paper system it won't be easily retrievable, but this is also the case if you use three or four different IT systems. Extracting a chronology for a case review would be hours of work, with plenty of room for error and omissions. In fact, we once installed our system in a school in Dorset where the paper safeguarding records had been held in the head teacher's office. A week before we arrived, he'd transferred them elsewhere for scanning and uploading into the system. In the intervening period, his office caught fire and everything in it was destroyed. Those safeguarding files had a lucky escape. Also, when you are adopting any IT system be very careful to check out where your data will be stored; is it in secure and resilient data centres or on the company's own servers? (We have encountered technology providers selling software to schools that was hosted on a computer at the home of one of the company's directors!). Also, has your software provider got all the industry-standard security accreditations? (We have seen a number of providers claiming these certifications when they don't actually hold it themselves. They use the fact that the data centre where they store your data has the certification to try and convince you that they do too.)

As with all things security related, you must balance safety with convenience. The more secure your system is, the less easy it may be for people to access; but the more accessible it is, the less secure it may be. If you're clear on what elements take priority in what circumstances, and have policies so everyone knows what the rules are, you have the foundations of a sound system. And when you're procuring any IT system for your organisation our best advice is always to involve specialist security and technical advisors (who may be your in-house staff or reputable external contractors).

Key learning points

- There are many legal aspects to consider when collecting, storing, accessing, and sharing data but the main ones are enshrined in the Data Protection Act 2018 and the GDPR. They provide a framework, not a bar, to processing personal data and special category data.
- Work with your DPO if you receive a subject access request and rely on their expertise for supporting you with how, when, and with whom you share personal data.
- The data protection principles and the Seven Golden Rules should be your guiding lights.
- Breaches of data security are an ever-present risk for every organisation; you should work with your DPO, your IT team, and any external software providers to ensure that your safeguarding data is secure and well protected.
- The vast majority of data breaches are committed by staff, often unwittingly, due to poor awareness and working practices.
- Regular staff training in relation to data protection, GDPR, and information security are essential.

Chapter 6
Strength through others

People and teams

How do you feel when you go home at the end of the day? Energised? Relaxed? Fulfilled? We hope this is often the case.

However, in a 2019 survey of teachers nearly three-quarters described themselves as 'stressed', and more than a third of education professionals said they had experienced a mental health issue in the past academic year.[1] Teachers were almost twice as anxious as most people, and were also feeling significantly more tearful on a regular basis. Two out of five reported having had difficulty concentrating, with around half experiencing sleep problems. And that was before Covid-19, the repeated lockdowns, remote learning, and 'long distance' safeguarding.

---

[1] D. Ferguson, 'Record levels of stress "put teachers at breaking point"'. *The Guardian*, 10 November 2019. Available from www.theguardian.com/education/2019/nov/10/stressed-teachers-at-breaking-point-says-report [accessed 17 December 2020].

We know that safeguarding is only part of this picture of pressure; the challenges you face every day are far more diverse than this one aspect of your role. We can't solve all your problems, but what we can do is to show you ways of making the safeguarding element of your job more straightforward through the way you work with the people and teams in your school.

Safeguarding is demanding – psychologically, emotionally, practically, and strategically. It brings you into contact with all sorts of complex and harrowing cases in which you have to work with children who have been victimised and those accused of doing the offending. That's why you need to see it not just as a set of tasks to be performed by you alone, but as a group responsibility with you at the helm, steering the way.

Dealing with this means understanding your role and those of the people supporting you; training and developing your team so everyone can fulfil their responsibilities competently; and paying attention to the much-neglected process of contingency planning. Together, these strategies will give you a far greater chance of low-stress success than you might be experiencing now.

Knowing who does what

Everyone in your setting should know that you are their safeguarding lead, and how they can contact you. The same applies to any deputy safeguarding leads you might have, as they also need to be accessible to staff if you're unavailable. You might also be supervising a team of people who have responsibility for various aspects of safeguarding, such as your school's Special Educational Needs Coordinator (SENCO), family liaison officer, or members of the pastoral team.[2] All members of staff should

---

[2] The introduction of the Special Educational Needs and Disability Regulations 2014 resulted in some people referring to the SENCO role as the SENDCo, albeit the regulations still refer to SENCOs and so do we. However, you can take your pick!

know about these roles, who performs them, and how to contact them. This is the type of basic information that should be covered in staff inductions, but can also be displayed on your school or college intranet and on posters in staff rooms.

The role of the safeguarding lead

When you were entrusted with this responsibility, you may not have been specifically tested on your suitability for safeguarding in an interview or assessment process. That's not to say that you don't have the attitude, aptitude, skills, and abilities to perform well in the role, and in some settings you'll be the only and obvious choice for it. Congratulations if you've managed to succeed in a demanding responsibility that might be no more than one line in your job description.

There's precious little guidance on what qualities a safeguarding lead should have. In Annex B of KCSIE 2020, there's a description of what a safeguarding lead ought to *do* and the tasks they should perform. For instance, they're expected to take lead responsibility for safeguarding, managing referrals, and working with others such as external agencies, the head teacher (if the head teacher isn't the lead themselves), and other staff. They should also keep up to date with their training, ensure staff are suitably trained, understand data protection law, and know enough to do their job well. The safeguarding lead is also expected to know how to deal with the many hundreds (and there *are* hundreds) of different safeguarding risks and scenarios that could arise. And that's without their other responsibilities such as raising awareness of safeguarding within the school, transferring child protection files when a child leaves, and being available to talk to staff, parents, and children about safeguarding whenever needed.

As you can see, this guidance doesn't describe the *competencies* required for the role; it simply gives a list of role-related tasks. What makes an excellent safeguarding lead? How can you identify a promising candidate for the role? What should you be looking out for, and be aware of in yourself, if you're asked to take on these duties? To help fill the gap in the official guidance, we've created a job description and competency framework for the role of safeguarding lead that we think you'll find useful. You can use it to identify gaps in your current job description, or maybe to self-review your own performance. And if you're recruiting or managing a safeguarding lead you can use the framework to inform those processes too. You'll find it here: https://safeguarding.thesafeguardingcompany.com/jd.

Mapping out the roles and responsibilities involved, both for yourself as leader and for the staff who help you, is the only way you'll gain clarity on the situation. When you do that, what was once confusing and unclear becomes simple. Then, after you have a handle on who should be doing what, you can capture it in a role description and person specification. This means that everyone knows what they should be focusing on, which can be a considerable weight off your mind.

After this, consider how you can assess your team's performance in both a supportive and a 'holding to account' kind of way. How can you help them to perform really well? What training and development opportunities can you provide? And what support do you have to do this?

Monitoring individual performance is especially challenging when much of your work is done on case work that's confidential in nature. This is most often the case if you're a head teacher because your 'line manager' is your governing body, CEO, or executive head. It's rarely appropriate for a governor or trustee to know about your cases (although this might be necessary if your governing body has to deal with a formal complaint that relates to a safeguarding case). Even if it's not a situation that involves special category data, it wouldn't be right for someone who's a member of the local community to have access to private information about a child's family life. Below, we suggest a way of managing this issue and improving your performance at the same time.

Supervision

The missing link is supervision. What do we mean by this? A helpful way of thinking about it is described by Penny Sturt and Jo Rowe in their book *Using Supervision in Schools*.[3] In it they describe four aspects of supervision that are all relevant to the role of the safeguarding lead:

o   competent performance (are you fulfilling the requirements of your role and in accordance with your line manager's expectations?);
o   continuing professional development (could you improve what you are doing if given some training or different opportunities?);
o   personal support (what support do you need? What would help you emotionally to do your job better?); and
o   engaging with the school (are you behaving and performing your role in a way that your manager and your employer would expect you to?).

Your line manager will supervise you in your role as safeguarding lead and make a judgement about your competence. Are you meeting their expectations of you in your role? Do they review your performance specifically in relation to your safeguarding role, and do they give you regular feedback? Remember, they're there to coach you too; having someone who supports you and who you can turn to for advice can really help. This can be particularly powerful in a MAT or school cluster, where a senior lead for safeguarding is in place.

---

[3] P. Sturt and J. Rowe, *Using Supervision in Schools: A Guide to Building Safe Cultures and Providing Emotional Support in a Range of School Settings*. Pavilion, 2018.

A line manager can also support you with confidential casework and enable you to improve your professional practice; this can be reassuring for them too. And if you're a head teacher yourself, consider delegating the role of safeguarding lead to someone else. This might seem like a radical step but think about how much more useful you can be in a line management role than if you're hands-on all the time. You would also be providing someone else with a development opportunity by passing on your knowledge, skills, and experience and using it as part of your succession planning.

In terms of continuing professional development, as the safeguarding lead you clearly have a responsibility to find the right development opportunities for yourself and for all the staff in your school or college. Your line manager and your governing body also have important roles to play in ensuring that you have the time and resources to make this happen.

Emotional support

An important aspect of supervision is emotional support, and the lack of this in safeguarding is something that concerns safeguarding leads greatly. This type of support should be delivered by someone with the right training and experience. Given the level of confidentiality required, it may be helpful if it's provided by someone other than your line manager. However, it's not only safeguarding leads who are left to handle the stressful and traumatic aspects of the role on their own; it can also affect your deputy (if you have one), SENCOs, family liaison officers, and pastoral staff, as well as the other staff dealing with safeguarding issues (which can range from classroom practitioners to school receptionists). You clearly have a role to play in ensuring they have the emotional support they need. It seems inconceivable that the sort of framework that supports people in other professions isn't routinely available to school and college staff involved in safeguarding, as if you're supposed to be able to deal with all the taxing stuff that comes your way without there being a serious impact on you. It's not as if safeguarding is the only pressure you have to deal with; you have the demands of your teaching role (if you're a teacher), dealing with child behaviour issues, and all the other aspects of the job. This isn't sustainable and we need to start thinking differently about how people are supported.

We need to reiterate that in England there's a clear requirement contained in *Working Together to Safeguard Children* for all safeguarding practitioners to have access to supervision. It's not an optional extra. It was also in a consultation draft for KCSIE 2020 but it was removed prior to publication (and it has not re-appeared in the KCSIE consultation draft for September 2021).[4] However, there is every likelihood that it will make it into KCSIE at some stage, and in any event it's good practice irrespective of whether it appears in statutory guidance, so if you don't already have supervision in place, now would be a great time to start.

Tenure of the safeguarding lead

Another aspect of safeguarding practice that we're concerned about is how long safeguarding leads are expected to stay in that role, because often this isn't the case in other professions. For instance, police child protection officers and staff who work for the police viewing illegal pornographic images for evidential purposes are required to have regular psychological support, and are only kept in their roles for a set period of time. Yet safeguarding leads, who are dealing with distressing cases day in day out, rarely receive that level of mandatory support, whether it be through occupational health or psychological services. If you're a head teacher, you can be the safeguarding lead for many years if you don't remove yourself from the position and supervise someone

---

[4] See https://consult.education.gov.uk/safeguarding-in-schools-team/keeping-children-safe-in-education-schools-and-col/supporting_documents/Proposed%20keeping%20children%20safe%20in%20education%20guidance%202021%20%20for%20consultation.pdf [accessed 18 January 2021]

else instead. Unless you have a switched-on line manager who makes sure you're supported, you could be exposed to harrowing safeguarding cases for years on end.

A final note on the practical application of supervision and how it can support educators. In the United States, there is a fast-growing interest in social and emotional learning (SEL) for children and adults.[5] A report published in 2020 by the Wallace Foundation and the RAND Corporation focused in part on developing the capacity of educators to deliver SEL to their students, and their conclusion was clear: the key to improving students' social and emotional skills is to start with the adults.[6] The report concludes that all school and college staff (not just teachers) should pay attention to their own wellbeing and to their own social and emotional capabilities before they attempt to develop those competencies in their students. They also recommend that any new social-emotional learning initiatives should include specific elements focused on building the SEL skills of the adults who are going to deliver these programmes.

Training and development

Once you have a team in place and you're clear on everyone's roles and responsibilities, it's time to think about training and development, including your and your team's ongoing needs. When everyone understands who's responsible for what, it

---

[5] SEL is defined as 'the process through which children and adults understand and manage emotions, set and achieve positive goals, feel and show empathy for others, establish and maintain positive relationships, and make responsible decisions'. H. L. Schwartz et al., *Early Lessons from Schools and Out-of-School Time Programs Implementing Social and Emotional Learning*, 2020. Available from www.wallacefoundation.org/knowledge-center/Documents/Early-Lessons-Schools-OST-Programs-SEL.pdf#page=1&zoom=auto,401,259 [accessed 17 December 2020].

[6] Schwartz et al., *Early Lessons from Schools and Out-of-School Time Programs Implementing Social and Emotional Learning*, 2020.

becomes much easier to identify each person's individual training and development needs. For instance, a governor will have a different set of requirements to a teacher, and to you.

Accessing appropriate training of a high standard can be a particular challenge because, as we've mentioned before, much of the safeguarding training we've seen (whether internal or from local authorities) is variable in quality. Often all it amounts to is a presenter clicking through countless slides crammed with statistical information that's of no practical use, and that gives no tool kit for delegates when they return to school. The sessions are often in the afternoon or evening when everyone is tired and just wants to go home (albeit, due to Covid-19, these are all now online), and there's no independent learning or competency assessment involved. We've both sat through many of these sessions as school governors, and gained no information about the role of the safeguarding governor or how the issues might affect school or college staff.

To make matters worse, due to reduced local authority budgets the amount of safeguarding training, advice, and support from them has plummeted. And while some of the commercially available training is high quality the standard can be variable, not least because there are no nationally agreed minimum qualifications or experience required before someone can set themselves up as safeguarding trainer. There are also no common standards for training content, delivery, or assessment. The reality is that across the country, safeguarding training is delivered by an enormous number of safeguarding consultants (mostly self-employed individuals or micro-companies who come from a wide range of backgrounds and with a variety of experiences), who are delivering safeguarding training to school and college staff in the absence of a common syllabus, agreed standards, or specific qualifications. It's important that your training is rigorous, has some element of assessment for those who attend, and that you can measure its impact. After all, it's costly in terms of both time and money, so you want to make sure it's effective.

Inconsistent training also affects how frontline staff are briefed on the signs and symptoms of abuse. What level of competence should you expect of staff if you can't evaluate the training they have received?

There's also a wide range of issues to cover in addition to what you might traditionally think of as safeguarding, such as information sharing, legalities in relation to certain types of issues such as FGM and Prevent, and people's statutory duties. Always be asking your staff, 'What do you need from me, as a leader, to help you with all of the tricky issues that safeguarding throws up? How can I help you to do a better job?' And make sure you measure how they're applying the training.

Safeguarding in international schools

The establishment of a safeguarding culture can be a particular problem in overseas English-medium international schools which inevitably have an internationally diverse teaching staff and pupil cohort, coming from many cultures and with different perspectives on safeguarding. The situation can be further complicated by the fact that staff performing support roles in international schools, such as in catering or grounds maintenance, may be from the local indigenous community. They might also be used to a different cultural and legal framework regarding issues like safeguarding, child protection, equality and diversity; not have English as a first language; and not understand what 'safeguarding' is, let alone what they should do when they encounter a concern. There is a critical need for the safeguarding training in these schools to establish a shared understanding and common standards for safeguarding, as well as clear systems and processes for raising and managing concerns.

Introducing safeguarding standards

We mentioned the lack of standards in training earlier, but it's also worth noting that there's no such thing as a standard for safeguarding as a whole. In other words, there's no common way of thinking about safeguarding that applies across all organisations which have safeguarding responsibilities, over and above the frameworks used by inspection bodies. When you think about it, there are commonly recognised international standards for all sorts of things: quality management and information security, for instance. But not for safeguarding. For us as a company it is vital that we hold ISO 27001, the internationally recognised standard for information security management and we'd like to see that same level of accreditation available for safeguarding.

Because there's no overarching standard, there's no way for an organisation to gain a formal accreditation to show it's been scrutinised over its approach to safeguarding. Nor is there any way for a safeguarding lead to show they've reached an appropriate level of competence. Without standards, how do you know what to aim for? It's hard to pinpoint what level of knowledge each person should have without understanding the overall standard you're wanting to achieve. This isn't the case in other areas of teaching, special educational needs being a good example. To become a SENCO, you have to go on an intensive course and put yourself through a development process with a pass or fail outcome. You also have to achieve a National Award in Special Educational Needs Co-ordination within three years of your appointment as a SEN teacher; this takes up to two years to complete, with a specific number of attendances required. There's even a national organisation for SENCOs called NASEN – the National Association for Special Educational Needs. NASEN has been around for over 25 years, supporting practitioners and keeping them up to date as well as delivering training. But there's none of this for a safeguarding lead – and that doesn't make sense to us.

In our view, postgraduate certifications and national (even international) standards are what the safeguarding profession ought to be driving towards. We'd love to see common standards and qualifications for safeguarding in the same way as, for instance, the health and safety industry.

The closest we have to a standard in England is the Ofsted inspection framework, which sets out what education inspectors are looking for. Here's some useful information extrapolated from Ofsted's 2019 guidance for inspectors.[7] (Other school inspection bodies in the UK – Estyn in Wales,[8] Education Scotland,[9] the Education and Training Inspectorate in Northern Ireland,[10] and the Independent Schools Inspectorate (ISI) – each have their own inspection standards.)

Inspection frameworks

Ofsted looks for an 'effective culture of safeguarding', focused on three core areas.

o   Are leaders and staff identifying children at risk of harm, or who have been harmed?

---

[7] Ofsted, *School Inspection Handbook*, November 2019. Available from https://assets.publishing.service.gov.uk/government/uploads/system/uploads/attachment_data/file/843108/School_inspection_handbook_-_section_5.pdf [accessed 17 December 2020].

[8] Estyn, 'Inspection guidance'. Available from www.estyn.gov.wales/inspection-process/inspection-guidance?sector=All [accessed 17 December 2020].

[9] Education Scotland, 'Our inspection frameworks'. Available from https://education.gov.scot/education-scotland/what-we-do/inspection-and-review/standards-and-evaluation-framework/05-our-inspection-frameworks/ [accessed 17 December 2020].

[10] Education and Training Inspectorate. Available from www.etini.gov.uk [accessed 17 December 2020].

o   What timely action do they take, and how well do they work with other agencies? Do leaders and staff always act in the best interests of the child?

o   How do responsible bodies and other staff manage their statutory responsibilities, and in particular, safer recruitment and allegations about staff?

To judge whether this is the case in your school, Ofsted wants to see evidence that:

o   policies, procedures, and other key documents comply with the statutory guidance;

o   all staff recognise and respond appropriately to risk;

o   leaders and staff understand their roles and responsibilities;

o   pupils are safe, educated, and aware;

o   pupils' behaviour is well managed; and

o   the school environment is safe for pupils, staff, and visitors.

It's also worth knowing what safeguarding information the inspectors want to see by 8:00am on the first day of the inspection. They'll ask for:

o   access to the Single Central Record;

o   a list of concerns, including information about which ones were referred to the local authority and how they were resolved;

o   details of pupils who have open cases with children's services, and for whom there's a multi-agency plan; and

o   records and analyses of exclusions, pupils taken off roll, behaviour incidents, use of internal isolation, sexual harassment or violence, and bullying, discriminatory, and prejudiced behaviour.

So far so good, but what would lead Ofsted to believe your safeguarding arrangements were inadequate? Ofsted is clear that it's if:

o   your school doesn't meet the statutory requirements or shows a serious cause for concern;

o allegations about staff are not handled properly;
o pupils don't feel safe at school;
o pupils don't feel confident that staff will help;
o pupils are frequently missing from school and this isn't addressed;
o bullying, peer-on-peer abuse, or discrimination is common; or
o leaders and staff don't adequately protect children from radicalisation and extremism.

You can see how specific these requirements are, and they're not theoretical. Some schools do fail their Ofsted inspections due to safeguarding issues alone. Between September and November 2019, Ofsted published 49 inspection reports with an overall effectiveness rating of 'inadequate', of which almost half were judged to have 'ineffective safeguarding'. Our analysis shows that the top three safeguarding issues that caused schools to fail the safeguarding element of their inspections were:

o governance;
o response to risk or harm; and
o systems and recording.

Inspection case studies

It's important to learn from our own mistakes but it's also important (and it somehow feels less challenging) to learn from the mistakes of others! Here are a number of Ofsted reports that highlight the issues inspectors have identified in schools that have failed to meet safeguarding requirements.

From a primary school in Hampshire:
Statutory safeguarding requirements have not been met. In particular:

o Not all staff have received, read or understood the latest statutory safeguarding guidance.

o Leaders have recruited new staff without having completed the statutory safer recruitment training.

o The Single Central Record of recruitment checks was incomplete at the time of the inspection.

o Staff have received basic safeguarding training, but their knowledge of key aspects is not strong. Some members of staff do not know who they should refer concerns about pupils' safety to.

And from a secondary school in Birmingham:

o School leaders do not ensure that all pupils feel safe at the school. Pupils, especially those in key stage 3 and pupils with SEND, feel unsafe at the school, due to the poor behaviour and incidents of bullying.

o Pupils have expressed concerns that, even when staff address one issue, another problem starts shortly afterwards. About a quarter of parents and care givers who responded to Ofsted's Parent View questionnaire said that the behaviour of pupils at the school is a concern and that their child does not feel safe at the school.

o Bullying is cited as a major factor for why they do not feel safe.

This makes for grim reading. We're aware of a large secondary school in the east of England which had outstanding academic results and exemplary pupil behaviour; the staff were excellent and had a great relationship with the local community. However, the school had a significant problem with drug dealers coming onto the campus, which the school had failed to address because it didn't want to admit it had a problem. The result? It failed its whole Ofsted inspection and was found to be 'Inadequate'. Following a re-inspection some months later, Ofsted found the school was still denying it had a problem, not least by failing to co-operate with local agencies. It was given a formal notice to improve.

In the absence of any other standards, you can use the relevant inspection requirements for your school as a basis for your training syllabus. How could you achieve a 100% pass rate in all these areas through the way you brief, train, and develop your team?

Contingency planning

If you've been in safeguarding for a while, you'll have noticed the types of incidents you're asked to deal with growing ever more diverse. Safeguarding used to be narrowly focused on child protection, but now it encompasses a vast range of issues that not only schools but other organisations such as local authorities, housing departments, and hospitals encounter on a daily basis. How can you instantly know the right approach to dealing with a sexting incident, a child with an anxiety attack, or a report of radicalisation? How can you possibly have expertise in all these fields? Being clear on the difference between what you always need to hold in your head, and what you can seek advice on (and who to ask or where to get it) is a key part of your role – because you can't know it all. In fact, you should acknowledge that you definitely *don't* know it all. Different issues have their own contexts and nuances, and if you don't handle them in the right way at the beginning you could make them worse.

You never know what's coming around the corner. In a previous chapter, we described an example of a complex scenario in which an allegation of sexual assault was made by one pupil against another. You can hardly imagine a more difficult situation to manage. Naturally, you'd let the police tackle the criminal aspects of the case, but how would you manage the pupils? Or what if an eight-year-old girl returned from an overseas holiday seeming withdrawn, and you had reason to believe she may have undergone FGM? How would you find out if your suspicions had justification, given the potential ramifications for the school's relationship with her parents if your concerns were unfounded?

'Duty of care' and negligence

This is where an understanding of the 'duty of care' principle is so important. This is a test in law that's often used in inquests and negligence claims against health trusts (and could easily be used against a school or college in a safeguarding case). Bizarrely, it originated from a legal case brought by a woman called May Donoghue in 1932.[11] She had drunk a bottle of ginger beer from a cafe that had the remains of a snail in it, and subsequently came down with stomach pains which were diagnosed as gastroenteritis and shock. As the law stood, Donoghue couldn't take legal action over the snail but a solicitor called Walter Leechman took up her case against the beer maker. It went all the way to the House of Lords, where Leechman argued that a manufacturer who puts a product on the market in a form that doesn't allow the consumer to examine it before using it is liable for any damage caused. In May 1932, Judge Lord Atkin of Aberdovey found in favour of Donoghue and gave the following address:

> The rule that you are to love your neighbour becomes in law, 'You must not injure your neighbour'... You must take reasonable care to avoid acts or omissions which you can reasonably foresee would be likely to injure your neighbour.

And with that the modern law of negligence was born. The term 'loving thy neighbour' can now be applied widely to any relationship in which a duty of care is owed. It encompasses personal injury, product liability, and professional negligence. But as a safeguarding lead, who are your 'neighbours'? They're the people who are, in the words of the law, 'so closely and directly affected by your actions that you ought reasonably to have them in contemplation as being so affected when you're directing your mind to the acts and omissions which are called into question'.

[11] C. Coleman, 'The legal case of the snail found in ginger beer'. *BBC News*, 20 November 2009. Available from http://news.bbc.co.uk/1/hi/business/8367223.stm [accessed 17 December 2020].

This, by the way, is why it's important to record your decisions and the rationale for them, because not doing something (whether by omission or by making a positive decision to do nothing) can be just as important as taking action.

The principle of what you can reasonably foresee comes up time and again when talking about duty of care, and this duty is at the heart of the role of safeguarding lead. It's defined as a legal obligation to act in the best interests of others, not to cause harm, and to act within your own competence. You owe a duty of care to the children you support, to your colleagues, your employer, yourself, and to the public interest. In a practical sense, this means that it's your legal responsibility not to make a bad situation worse; not that you would ever intend to do this but it's not just a matter of doing a good job – it's also a legally binding condition of your work.

Scenario-based planning and training

A combination of complex scenarios and legal responsibilities is pretty daunting, but you can lighten the load considerably by undertaking some contingency planning. This has a dual purpose: to help you to cope with most situations that come your way, and to train your team. There's nothing worse than having to make it up as you go along when a tricky situation arises, and although you won't be able to prepare for every kind of incident, you can use your data to identify which might be the most likely issues to arise. Plus, your people will feel prepared and confident.

Essentially, contingency plans help you and your staff to discharge your duty of care. People are properly briefed so they can react in the right way, and risk is reduced. A plan can be a one-page document that outlines the key steps to take – in fact, the simpler the better. The last thing you need is to be wading through reams of paper when you have an urgent and difficult problem on your hands.

Here's an example of how you could run a hands-on contingency planning session that's useful for both training and groundwork.

You'll be pleased to know it doesn't involve any PowerPoint slides; all you need is an outline of a situation that you've prepared beforehand. Firstly, create a theoretical incident that starts off simple and straightforward, and give it the 'rising tide' treatment as the session goes on. Let's say it's a report of one child sexting another. At first it only involves two parties, but gradually it becomes clear that many pupils are doing it and that it's been going on for a few weeks. Now you have to decide whether to involve parents and the police. What's the legal basis for you sharing information about it? Next, you have an angry parent who has got wind of the story and is wanting to see you straightaway. How do you handle the conversation with them? And so on.

Or how about this one? A teacher has noticed that a child often comes into school smelling of cannabis, which suggests it's being smoked in their home. This creates a dilemma. There's a potential health impact on the child, and they're also being exposed to the use of an illegal drug. Drugs are often linked to other areas of criminality, so there's a risk from that as well. Who should the teacher tell, if anybody? If they report it to the police, the child's home might be searched and the parents arrested – this could be traumatic. If they don't tell the police they might decide to tell the parents, but that's one hell of an awkward conversation; the parents could be angry, which could also lead to harm to the child. The teacher could make a referral to children's social care, but there would be consequences from that too. There's no easy answer, but if you've planned ahead of time who the teacher should talk to and how they could deal with the situation, they'll be several steps ahead. You can see how these hands-on training sessions can generate useful contingency plans, which feel real and are thought-through because they've been created in as close to real-life situations as you can get.

Not only that, but they give your people the emotional preparation for the kinds of scenarios they may face, and enable them to air their worries. They learn what their powers and responsibilities are, when to ask for help, and where to seek it. If you don't deal with what's going on in their heads they'll become stressed and demotivated – you need to create a culture in which it's okay to talk about these things.

On one occasion we delivered a school safeguarding training session where a teacher asked us, 'If I report a safeguarding concern will the parents find out that I was the person who reported it?' Our answer was 'Yes, they might well discover that, but it's part of your job. In fact, it's your legal duty to report your concerns, even if the parents are angry with you and even when it's unpleasant. But remember that your head teacher and your governors are there to support you, and the police too, if you think there is a potential risk to your personal safety.' If we hadn't surfaced that anxiety it would have remained unsaid. He'd have been thinking, 'If I report this, what's the impact on me?' And that could have led to him keeping quiet about something he should have spoken up about.

We do acknowledge that at a local level, this kind of training is time consuming. Could every primary school develop its own contingency plans for dealing with every kind of incident? Clearly not, but there are some simple steps you can take and it's certainly an area that deserves your attention.

Safer recruitment

Putting in place robust procedures that identify and deter individuals who may pose a risk to children is a critical part of the safeguarding responsibilities of schools and colleges. This should begin with the recruitment process itself, as the first line of defence against potential perpetrators. It's essential that safeguarding leads understand the importance of this process, given that recruitment is sometimes seen as an administrative burden undertaken without the involvement of the safeguarding lead.

Currently there's no statutory guidance for safer recruitment in England, although the KCSIE 2020 draft consultation did include a section on the recruitment and selection process. Unfortunately, it was withdrawn before the publication of the final version in September 2020, but should still be considered as good practice.[12] Here's a summary of the highlights.

o All job adverts should clearly communicate the school or college's commitment to safeguarding and promotion of the welfare of children.

o Schools should set out the safeguarding requirements for the role advertised, making it clear that it's an offence to apply if the applicant is barred from regulated activity.

o The application form should ask for information about employment history (including the reasons for any gaps), references, and a personal statement detailing personal qualities and experience.

o In addition, shortlisted candidates should complete a self-declaration form which discloses any criminal history and any other information which may make them unsuitable to work with children.

o Named referees should be verified to make sure that references are genuine and have been authorised by an appropriate person.[13]

---

[12] These exact bullet points have now re-appeared in the consultation draft for KCSIE 2021. https://consult.education.gov.uk/safeguarding-in-schools-team/keeping-children-safe-in-education-schools-and-col/supporting_documents/Proposed%20keeping%20children%20safe%20in%20education%20guidance%202021%20%20for%20consultation.pdf [accessed 18 January 2021]

[13] We're aware of a recent example in international schools, when at the end of the school year 38 members of staff left a particular school to take up new jobs in other international schools and not one enquiry or reference request was made to the school they had recently left.

All these measures are designed to set the bar high when it comes to the recruitment process. In particular, they encourage schools to check out the background details of every applicant thoroughly, especially where there are unexplained gaps or information that doesn't quite add up. The insistence on self-declaration isn't a statutory requirement at this stage, but it's an effective deterrent for people who may have something to hide.

The Single Central Record

The Single Central Record is another cornerstone of the safer recruitment process in schools and colleges, and there are strict statutory guidelines for educational settings in each of the UK nations (albeit the terminology may vary). The Single Central Record is a register of the pre-appointment checks that schools and colleges in England and Wales undertake when they recruit people into roles, including governors and trustees and anyone who carries out regulated activity.

What is interesting is that in many schools and colleges the safeguarding lead appears to have little to do with the Single Central Record, with the responsibility often sitting with business managers/bursars, HR staff, administrators, and school receptionists rather than with the safeguarding lead. This seems somewhat odd given that the relevant statutory requirements are to be found within KCSIE, and that safer recruitment and the Single Central Record should be a central pillar of safeguarding. While the maintenance of the Single Central Record itself may be an administrative task that can be delegated, it is essential that you as the safeguarding lead are involved in establishing and monitoring the safer recruitment process, not least for staff induction and the provision of relevant training for those involved in staff selection.

Without exception, inspection bodies will spend a considerable amount of time scrutinising the Single Central Record; it's usually the first thing that inspectors examine on the first morning of an inspection. We've heard it described by some safeguarding leads as a 'forensic examination'. So it's critically important that entries are up to date and accurate. If any significant errors or omissions are found, it's likely that your safeguarding practice could be judged as ineffective.

The checks undertaken as part of the Single Central Record process can vary depending on the type of role the person is applying for, but can include the following:

o   verification of identity;
o   Disclosure and Barring Service (DBS) and barred list check;[14]
o   checks on prohibitions, sanctions, and restrictions;
o   Section 128 management check;
o   relevant teaching qualifications;
o   right to work in the UK;
o   checks on applicants who have lived or worked overseas;
o   childcare disqualification checks;
o   references; and
o   fitness to work.

It's worth bearing in mind that staff performance in relation to safeguarding beyond the recruitment phase can often be overlooked. In the police service, initial employment vetting is followed up by regular re-vetting, known as 'aftercare'. However, there are some restrictions on doing this in teaching albeit there is an 'update service' available and when a staff member moves to another school the new employer will have to undertake its own safer recruitment process and record all the pre-employment checks in its own Single Central Record. As the safeguarding lead it's essential that you maintain an overview of the performance

---

[14] Checks for names of individuals who are barred from taking part in the management (which includes senior management and governance) of any independent school in England and Wales and in locally maintained schools in England only.

and behaviour of all staff and other relevant people (such as governors, trustees, and contractors) in relation to safeguarding once they are in post or working in your school.

Identifying offenders

It's when someone is actually working in your setting that your safeguarding system can provide you with significant insights into their attitude towards safeguarding, and it's important that you're vigilant for the 'signs and symptoms' that might indicate that you actually have an offender in your midst. Because for a number of reasons, pupils and families may not come forward with complaints.

Some of the most notorious paedophiles in education have been expert at grooming not only their victims but also parents, fellow staff members, and even whole communities, often for many years. One such individual was Ralph Morris.

Case study – Ralph Morris

Ralph Morris was the principal and joint owner of Castle Hill Independent Special School in Ludlow, Shropshire.[15] The school catered for children who had been placed there by local authorities across the country (including several London boroughs) because their particular needs could not be met closer to home. Morris was seen as a bastion of the local community, was a regular church-goer, and appeared to be a friend to everyone, not least the local police (Morris actually arranged for the local police to give water safety lessons to his pupils in the school's private swimming pool). Indeed, such was his status within the community that he was able to establish a board of governors comprised of 'the great and the

---

[15] The Needle [blog], 'Ralph Morris: Castle Hill report'. Available from https://theneedleblog.wordpress.com/2013/05/30/ralph-morris-castle-hill-report/ [accessed 17 December 2020].

good' both from the local town and further afield. Except Morris wasn't a pillar of society or anyone's friend – he was a predatory paedophile.

When Morris was finally arrested, I was the custody officer who authorised Morris's detention. Probably because of the unusual nature of the case, I have a vivid memory of escorting him to his cell; I was wearing a short-sleeved shirt and recall him touching me on my forearm, saying, 'I wouldn't do anything to hurt them, you know.' Why he said that to me I don't know, but I remember looking into his eyes and seeing a man who appeared weak and pleading, but who had both the cunning and the capability to commit the most awful acts of abuse on children who were already hugely vulnerable.

In April 1991, Morris was convicted at Shrewsbury Crown Court of multiple counts of buggery, indecent assault, and assault occasioning actual bodily harm. During the investigation, 106 young men from local authority areas across the country, who had all at one time attended the school, were jointly interviewed by police officers and social workers. Many said they didn't come forward at the time because Morris's standing in the community was such that they didn't think they would be believed. And they were right – several pupils had previously made allegations to the police that had been discounted.

But surely someone else in the school must have known or suspected something? A teacher, perhaps? A clue to what might have been going on can be found in the fact that one of Morris's staff members, John Duggan, had previously been head teacher of another special school but had been sacked (albeit not convicted) following allegations of sexual misconduct, and yet Morris had employed him. Following Morris's conviction, Duggan was convicted of indecent assault against a former pupil and perverting the course of justice.

Sadly, there are many other similar cases, including the systematic sexual abuse perpetrated by staff on very young children at

Ashdown House School in East Sussex. In his book *Stiff Upper Lip*, and in his subsequent documentary, journalist and broadcaster Alex Renton describes the sexual abuse perpetrated against him by his teacher when Alex was only eight years old (a day that he described as 'the end of my childhood').[16] Other former pupils from the school disclosed similar abuse at the hands of their teachers, often with the complicity of the school and, at times, parents.

Case study – William Vahey

A shocking contemporary example of the failure of recruitment and vetting processes in education settings is the notorious case of William Vahey, which was the subject of a 2016 Serious Case Review.[17] Vahey was a US citizen convicted in 1969 in California of sex offences towards young boys, which resulted in a 90-day jail sentence and five years' probation. Despite his conviction, Vahey qualified as a teacher in the United States in 1972, and over the following 42 years was employed in ten English-medium international schools in Europe, the Middle East, the Far East, and South America, none of which spotted the 1969 conviction. Between 2009 and 2013, Vahey worked at the Southbank International School in London before moving to a school in Nicaragua, where a USB thumb drive belonging to him was found to contain hundreds of photographs depicting the sexual abuse of school-age children. This led to Vahey being interviewed by the FBI and admitting a number of offences. However, before the FBI enquiries could be completed Vahey committed suicide in Minnesota on 21 March 2014. The evidence uncovered during that investigation showed that Vahey had been a predatory paedophile

---

[16] *Boarding Schools: The Secret Shame – Exposure* (ITV), 2018. Available from www.youtube.com/watch?v=uhWOM3iqF7c [accessed 17 December 2020].

[17] J. Wonnacott, *Serious Case Review: Southbank International School*. Available from www.rbkc.gov.uk/pdf/Southbank%20SCR%20REPORT%2012%20 1%2016.pdf [accessed 17 December 2020].

who had systematically sexually abused pupils in the schools at which he worked.

Abuse in schools today

Unfortunately, there will always be voices who claim that this type of abuse is historical and is no longer happening. We know this not to be true, and if you have any doubt about this take note of the words of Chief Constable Simon Bailey, the national police lead for child protection, when he was interviewed in 2018 for Alex Renton's documentary: 'Abuse in schools is the most prolific form of institutional abuse that officers around the country are investigating. It's almost double that of any other form of institutional abuse.' Furthermore, a Freedom of Information request sent to UK police forces by the makers of the documentary revealed that between 2012 and 2017, no fewer than 425 people were accused of sexual attacks at boarding schools and 160 people were charged as a consequence.

The most recent and authoritative source of evidence in relation to child sexual abuse in schools or colleges in the UK is the *Truth Project Thematic Report* published in December 2020 by the Independent Inquiry into Child Sexual Abuse.[18] The report describes the experiences of nearly 700 victims and survivors of child sexual abuse that occurred between the 1940s and 2010s in schools or colleges, or was perpetrated by a member of staff who worked in them, or by other students. Here are just some of the findings of the research:

1. The majority of perpetrators reported by participants sexually abused in the context of schools were male teachers or other educational staff.

---

[18] Independent Inquiry into Child Sexual Abuse, *Truth Project Thematic Report: Child Sexual Abuse in the Context of Schools*, December 2020. Available from www.iicsa.org.uk/document/truth-project-thematic-report-child-sexual-abuse-context-schools [accessed 15 January 2021].

2. Perpetrators often manipulated and groomed children, staff, and parents in order to facilitate sexual abuse, and often had good reputations with staff and parents, or were seen as 'cool' by pupils.

3. 15% of participants reported sexual abuse perpetrated by peers or older children, the second most frequently reported perpetrator type in the context of schools after teachers and educational staff.

4. Sexual abuse perpetrated in residential schools was disproportionately higher in accounts from Truth Project participants compared to the proportion of these types of schools in England and Wales, and the percentage of children who attended them.

5. Sexual abuse in independent and special schools was disproportionately higher in participants' accounts. There were also higher levels of physical and psychological abuse reported in these two school types, compared to state schools.

6. 54% of the participants sexually abused in state schools were female. Over 75% of participants sexually abused in independent and special schools were male.

7. 42% of participants sexually abused in the context of schools were aware of other victims of sexual abuse.

8. Participants also talked about suspicion or rumours in schools surrounding the perpetrators, resulting in many missed opportunities for safeguarding.

9. When participants disclosed sexual abuse during childhood, it was frequently to a person in authority within the institution.

10. In some cases, when participants were asked by parents or teachers whether they were being sexually abused, they denied the sexual abuse to protect the perpetrator and/or the environment the perpetrator created. (pages 2–4)

What does all this mean for you? It means that as a safeguarding lead you have a clear duty to be relentlessly vigilant in your protection of children, both from other children and from potential predators within your own establishment's staff. However unpalatable this may sound, it's a fundamental requirement of your role.

Key learning points

- Safeguarding can be very challenging, but it's much more manageable when you have a well-trained and competent team of people to help you.
- Make sure that the job descriptions of the safeguarding lead and any deputies are clearly defined and that their responsibilities are set out in detail.
- It's important for all staff to understand their duty of care and what that means for them.
- It is good practice to provide professional and emotional support ('supervision') for all safeguarding practitioners in your setting, including you!
- Contingency planning has the dual benefit of being an excellent training tool and a generator of realistic plans that you can use when needed.
- Safer recruitment is a critical first line of defence against people who may present significant risks to children.
- Never forget that the danger may lie within your own organisation – be relentlessly vigilant.

Chapter 7
Your safeguarding data universe
The rich picture

*I*t was a bright, sunny day in the south-west of England, and our mission was to meet the newly appointed head of a local primary school. The receptionist ushered us into his office and told us he would be along shortly. After a minute or two an energetic man in his forties bounded into the room, complete with PE shorts and whistle. The head teacher was clearly taking an active role in promoting healthy activities in his school. Good stuff!

'Afternoon!' he said. 'Sorry about the gear. Our Year 4 teacher is off sick so I had to cover, otherwise I'd have had a rebellion from the TA. You know how it is.'

Plonking himself down in a chair, he folded his arms and turned to face us.

'So, we're here to talk about safeguarding. Fire away.'

We needed little encouragement to discuss our favourite topic so we started by asking him a few simple questions, such as how many safeguarding concerns the school recorded in the average month and how many children he had with complex needs.

'No idea!' he replied cheerfully. 'It's all in there.'

Following the trajectory of his arm, we found ourselves staring at a grey filing cabinet. So far, so normal. With his safeguarding records languishing in cardboard folders, it was little wonder he didn't have any way of analysing his information other than on a child-by-child basis. He couldn't see the rich picture.

***

What do we mean by 'the rich picture'? To answer this, let's step back for a moment. As we discussed earlier, one of the most valuable – and challenging – things you can do in safeguarding is to identify emerging trends. This could be anything from a new social media platform that's causing issues (like when Snapchat first came on the scene), or a particular type of drug (as we saw with the synthetic drug 'Spice'). It could be a problem affecting one child, a number of siblings, a registration group, a year group, or the whole school. And it goes without saying that the sooner you spot what's going on, the more quickly you can get on top of it, and the more effectively you can minimise the harm and stop it spreading. If you wait until there's an emergency and react rather than prevent, the impact can be significantly worse and the problem become intractable.

But here's the thing. You can only do this prevention work by generating a rich picture. This is the overview of what's going on in your school both now and potentially in the future, presented to you from all sorts of useful angles. Being in possession of what the police call 'intelligence' turns you from being a first responder into a proactive safeguarder.

So how do you gain a view of the rich picture? Obviously, in a small establishment it's easier to identify emerging trends than it is in a larger one, but even then it's not a great idea for one person, such as a head teacher, to be holding this knowledge in their head. If they leave or hand over responsibility for safeguarding to someone else, it goes with them. The key is to have comprehensive data that you can analyse in whatever way you want. By child, by type of concern, by date range, by location, and by staff member – this is just a selection of what should be available to you. Because without good data how can you decide what action to take, let alone build a portrait over time of people, places, and types of concern?

Seeing the rich picture not only enables you to spot large-scale trends, but also to identify individual children who are vulnerable and at risk. And let's not forget the wider context in which concerns are reported. When you have the right information, you can think not only about how you support individuals but also what it means across your community and in children's social care, health services, and policing. Because if these issues are manifesting themselves in school, they'll also be evident outside it as well – one influences the other.

It's not as if schools are strangers to data. Academic data, for instance, indicates how individual pupils, registration groups, year groups, and other groups are likely to perform in exams, so you can put in place appropriate measures. Suppose a cohort of students looks likely to do badly in its GCSEs; this could be down to suppressed motivation, lower ability, or disruptive behaviour by a few. Your school can then take relevant action because it has the data that alerts it to the problem. There's also absence data, progress data, demographic data – schools are awash with the stuff. Safeguarding data is no less important and sometimes more so. After we've taken you through the enormous potential it holds, we hope you'll agree.

However, the rich picture isn't only made up of numerical data; it also consists of non-numerical, qualitative data. This is information that can be observed but often not measured. Qualitative data seeks to understand what happened from a human perspective, and comprises information recorded as a result of what people see, hear, discover, or are told. Just like numerical data it can be analysed, inferences drawn from it, and action taken. An example is the chronology recorded while managing a safeguarding concern, such as the language a child used to disclose abuse. Did the child give the same explanation every time an injury was caused? 'It was an accident; I fell over; I walked into a door.' You can see that the information isn't only to do with the number of times the abuse happened, but also the words used to describe it.

Sources of data

The primary source of your data is your own safeguarding concerns. However, this is made up of information that can come from a significant number of sources, including:

○ self-reporting by a pupil;

○ reporting by a pupil about another pupil;

○ drawings or written work by pupils;

○ concerns raised by families or caregivers about their own or other children;

○ reporting by staff, governors, contractors, volunteers, agency staff, peripatetic teachers, and visitors based on their own observations;

○ partner agency reporting, such as police reports of domestic violence in a child's home, or children's social care raising concerns about a child acting as a young carer;

○ alerts from other sources, such as software monitoring systems, that identify pupils accessing harmful material online;

○ CCTV systems, social media, audio and video recordings (often on pupils' own devices);

o   community members or other unconnected third parties; and

o   anonymous reporting.

You can see how you can gain a rich picture of what's going on in your setting and in your pupils' lives by collating all the information available to you. This will also help you to identify where there may be gaps in your knowledge, which you might be able to fill by asking another agency whether they have any relevant information about a child. Gathering data from different types of reporting can also be a helpful way of corroborating what you already have, and if the extra data shows a number of repeat incidents that you weren't already aware of this would signal a higher level of risk. (You will need to be particularly proactive in gathering data about pupils who are dual registered with other settings such as alternative provision or for those pupils who move from your school or college into a pupil referral unit or hospital school and subsequently return to your setting.)

You have to weigh up the information you receive, which isn't always easy, particularly when it comes from a 'non-professional' source or is anonymous, as people can have different motivations for raising concerns. Some do so out of malice, while others are well-meaning but turn out to be mistaken. For instance, it's more than possible for a parent to exaggerate or fabricate an issue if they're suffering from Munchausen's syndrome by proxy.[1] You have to take all these things into account when you assess the quality of the information you receive.

The infinite potential of data

There are a number of key things you can do with safeguarding data when you can organise and analyse it. For example you can:

[1] NHS, 'Fabricated or induced illness'. Available from www.nhs.uk/conditions/fabricated-or-induced-illness [accessed 17 December 2020].

Be proactive

This is one of the most important benefits of an electronic safeguarding system. Rather than different members of staff knowing different things and recording them on paper, where the records end up in a filing cabinet, you can analyse the data proactively. This is how you put the child at the centre of your considerations, so you can quickly see what's going on in their universe and give them early help if needed. You're not waiting until there's a significant problem in that child's life; you're identifying it before it becomes a crisis. In this case, having a prevention strategy goes from sounding like a good idea to becoming a reality, because how can you know what to prevent if you don't understand what's waiting around the corner?

Identify patterns and trends

Categorising the concerns you're managing helps you to be precise about the incident or issue. It also makes it easy to retrieve data quickly and to spot problems at an early stage. To have a reliable categorisation system means you controlling what the categories are and what kind of data should be entered under each; allowing staff to 'freestyle' their categories leads to inconsistencies. Remember: quality in means quality out.

Target resources effectively

If there's one thing all schools are short of, it's money. And if there's one thing all teachers lack, it's time. So anything that enables you to focus your resources efficiently and effectively has to be a good thing. Suppose your data analysis was to show a growing problem of drug dealing near the school. More worryingly, a couple of pupils have been approached by drug dealers, and it seems to happen most frequently on a Friday afternoon. You now have targeted options. You can inform the police, who now know they need to patrol the area on Fridays after school; you can talk about the topic in assemblies; and you can even introduce it into the curriculum. What you do about it is up to you, but whatever action you take you'll know it's highly targeted.

With a rich picture in front of you, not only will you use your resources wisely but you'll also be as sure as you can be that you're making the most effective use of your pupils' attention. Using lesson time to focus on issues that aren't a major concern is a waste of everyone's efforts. For instance, if your school is like most, you will at some stage teach your pupils how to use social media wisely. But unless you have the data that shows you which types of media are causing a problem (if any), you'll only be talking about it in a generic way. The children will see right through you. It's like you're 'sheep dipping' all the children with the same information, when you could be teaching them what they really need to know.[2]

This also relates to which children you target for what type of attention. Taking the drug-dealing example a stage further, if your data shows that the police have given warnings about County Lines activity in your area, you can put in place focused campaigns for the year groups (or individual children) most likely to be vulnerable to becoming involved. You'll only know what to do if you combine the internal and external data in your system to understand what the contextual issues are.

Work seamlessly with other agencies

Having an electronic system means you can extract information easily for communication with external agencies, such as the children's social care departments in local authorities. If you have the data to support your referral, and if it's in the right format for the agency in question, you're more likely to be successful.

---

[2] SWGfL – the South West Grid for Learning – is a charity that has a wide range of excellent tools, advice and resources that will provide you with all the information you will need: https://swgfl.org.uk

You can also use your data to analyse how many of your external referrals have been accepted or declined, such as when you refer children to your local authority's social care team. That way, you can understand why some referrals might not have met the threshold and, when appropriate, challenge those decisions.

Given how vital it is to share information with external agencies in order to prevent yet another tragedy, the importance of being able to extract the data you need easily and accurately can't be underestimated.

Communicate internally

Having access to the rich picture helps you to communicate with governors and other school leaders; they can then make informed decisions because you've given them the information in the right format for their needs. They now know what's going on, so they can set strategy and policies accordingly. You can also use it to justify additional safeguarding resources, because having the data to back up your business case is very powerful.

Manage performance

An important benefit of a safeguarding software system is that you can use it to improve your own performance as a safeguarding lead. Your data ought to give you a clear picture of what's working well, and of the lessons you've learned and what you've done to improve things. How many times have you taken a certain course of action, such as to refer a child to children's social care? How many times was it successful? And can you spot any trends in the data that would point to ways of gaining a better result in the future?

It can also be invaluable when it comes to managing the performance of other members of staff, as it shows you much about their attitude towards safeguarding. For instance, which staff are recording safeguarding concerns, and which aren't? Do some report everything, maybe because they don't have the confidence or understanding to handle minor issues themselves, while others never report anything because they don't think it's worthwhile? An effective system will allow you to analyse the content by staff member not just by child, so you will be able to identify any training and development needs. You can also monitor the type of interactions between staff and children, and any allegations made against staff by pupils or their families.

See the rich picture

A key component of good safeguarding is having professional curiosity, and never more so than when looking at the rich picture.[3] When you collect and use data consistently across different settings and over time, you're in a position to use it intelligently and to decide the who, what, when, where, why, and how of deciding what action to take (or not to take). We understand you don't have the resources to gather and analyse everything, and you may also have time constraints, but a bit of basic analysis can be transformative. You could even make it part of your curriculum. How about asking some maths pupils to look at the statistics at an anonymised level? It might give you something insightful to take to your governing body.

The rich picture isn't a flat image; it's a three-dimensional one that's constantly changing. Think of a child you're concerned about as a planet at the centre of their own universe. What's going on around them? What's their relationship with the other planets (peers, friends, family, and staff)? What do you know and, just as importantly, not know, in order to paint a rich picture? The

---

[3] Worcestershire Safeguarding Children Board Learning & Improvement Briefing Sheet 9, *Professional Curiosity – See Past the Obvious*. Available from www.safeguardingworcestershire.org.uk/wp-content/uploads/2019/03/Briefing-9-Professional-Curiosity.pdf [accessed 17 December 2020].

answers to these questions come from your data, and the need for the data applies equally to the other planets and to the whole of your safeguarding universe.

This logic operates at many levels: schools, clusters of schools, MATs, and local authorities – all need to consider the safeguarding issues affecting individuals and groups of pupils. There are various factors that contribute to the data: age, registration group, stage of education, gender, faith, family or other relationships, location, and many other needs and characteristics such as special needs, Pupil Premium, disabilities, looked after children, children in need, children in care, and more.

Collecting the right data

You'll have gathered by now that your safeguarding prevention strategy and activity should be informed by what you know, rather than assume. And what you know will be based on what data you've decided to collect, so it stands to reason that the rich picture springs ultimately from your data collection strategy.

Some years ago, the government introduced safeguarding audits for schools to submit to their local authorities.[4] If you've ever toiled into the evening to complete one of these, you won't need us to tell you how bureaucratic and time consuming they are. Answering questions such as, 'Provide evidence that your school has a commitment to inter-agency working', or 'How many referrals have you made to other agencies?' is no picnic. The audits can be anything up to 100 pages long, and it goes without saying that if all you have access to is a filing cabinet and a four-ring binder, they'll be almost impossible to complete.

---

[4] These are known as Section 157 or Section 175 audits. Sections 157 and 175 of the Education Act 2002 place a statutory duty on independent and maintained schools to make arrangements to ensure that in discharging their functions, they have regard to the need to safeguard and promote the welfare of children.

What has made matters worse is the lack of evidence about how local authorities and the former Local Safeguarding Children Boards use the resulting data to give comparative feedback to schools and colleges. Such feedback should certainly be helpful, giving you a way of comparing yourselves with others, but from what we're told by schools this rarely happens. The audit results just seem to disappear into the space–time continuum. The outcome is that some authorities have taken the decision to stop conducting audits because they're not doing anything with the data.

This is an excellent example of when people think that collecting information is important, but are not doing it the right way. For instance, most local authorities create their own audit questions rather than using a consistent template, which makes it almost impossible to analyse the data regionally or nationally. This shows that gaining a view of the rich picture requires you to give careful consideration to what your data requirements actually are. Have you made a conscious decision about what you need to collect, in what format, and how?

The risks of incomplete record keeping in relation to child sexual abuse (CSA) were starkly revealed in a research report published in September 2020 by the Centre of Expertise on Child Sexual Abuse.[5] The study set out to build a better understanding of the scale of CSA encountered by local authority children's services in Wales, and to explore how concerns regarding CSA are identified, recorded, and responded to. Two of the key findings of the research were that:

---

[5] Centre of Expertise on Child Sexual Abuse, *Responding to Child Sexual Abuse: Learning from Children's Services in Wales*. Available from www.csacentre.org.uk/documents/responding-to-csa-childrens-services-wales-briefing/ [accessed 3 January 2021].

1. the scale of child sexual abuse concerns encountered by local authority children's services is significantly under-reported in official data;

2. while much information is recorded about the nature and context of CSA, important details are often missing and data is difficult to access and analyse.

Although it should go without saying, it has to be said that the data you and your staff record and report to your local authority could have a fundamental impact on the protection of children from child sexual abuse. The systems, processes, and training that you provide for your staff are fundamental to achieving high-quality data, as is the quality of your relationship with your local authority.

Organising your data

Until relatively recently, if you'd have walked past a certain meeting room in Weymouth on a particular day in July, you'd have witnessed an interesting sight. It would have been a group of local primary school safeguarding leads handing over their records (contained within brown cardboard folders) to their secondary school equivalents. The latter would, in a time-honoured ritual, solemnly sign a receipt to confirm they'd received the said folders. What was in them? Nobody really knew. There was no list of contents, no initialling of each page to signify receipt, and no idea if anything had been removed or destroyed prior to handover. What's more, the data within each folder had been recorded in a different way because there wasn't (and still isn't) a nationally recognised, common requirement for the recording of safeguarding information. As a result, there was no reliable record of the information shared between the schools, or of whether it complied with data protection legislation. Fortunately, these schools now use an electronic system so this is no longer an issue; they can transfer their safeguarding records safely and securely between themselves, and can instantly read and understand those sent to them. The audit trails within the system track the information shared, and record who did what and when.

Looking beyond data, it's common for primary schools to talk to secondary schools and for secondary schools to talk to colleges about pupils who are moving between settings. Exam results and behavioural issues are discussed for individual children and groups, with the result that the transfer is easier than it would have been without the communication. If this applies to academic issues, it ought to apply to safeguarding too. Children who have problems at home, mental health issues, or other issues to deal with deserve to have their needs recognised alongside their test results. This is often done informally but there's no common framework for it, just in the same way that there's no agreed system for moving safeguarding data around the education network. This lack of consistency and clarity knocks a hole in the rich picture because the data requirement isn't laid out. Of course, this isn't under your direct control, but you can do something about it on a local level by giving careful thought to how you collect your own information.

What's more, it's worth thinking about what you want to achieve with this data when you have it. When we were in the police service, we worked with what's called the national intelligence model, which was excellent. Its purpose was to set strategic direction, make prioritised and defendable resourcing decisions, formulate plans, and manage risks. In essence, these are the key elements that should inform your safeguarding data requirement, because your data should enable you to do all these things.

Working with others

Once you start thinking about the potential for the data you collect, the sky's the limit. When a dozen schools in Tameside, Greater Manchester, pooled their absence data to look for trends, they discovered a dip in attendance among disadvantaged pupils on one particular day of the year: 14 December. The teachers scratched their heads over the date, but a quick online search revealed that this was Christmas Jumper Day. They realised that while these days were fun for many children, they were humiliating for those who couldn't afford to buy a Christmas jumper. Immediately, the schools took the day off the calendar. Another of their findings was that a two-week Whitsun holiday taken by local primary schools (but not secondaries) reduced the attendance of older siblings, who might go on family holidays or have to look after their younger brothers and sisters at home.[6]

These examples give a glimpse of what's possible when you harness the potential of collaborative information. Have you thought about approaching local schools to see if you can share anonymised data? You could use it to monitor and benchmark all sorts of things, such as behavioural concerns in certain year groups or a rise in referrals to children's social care. And instead of each school designing its own approach to an issue, you could come up with something you can all work with. It's incredibly useful to know whether your school is recording more or fewer concerns than others, and to reflect on whether that's a good or a bad thing. The day you discover an emerging trend across your area that you wouldn't have known about if you'd only focused on your own school will be the day you experience the true power of the rich picture.

Key learning points

- Your data should be a key strategic asset in preventing and reducing harm.
- Having a data strategy helps you to use your information to enhance your safeguarding practice

---

[6] M. George, 'Exclusive: Data reveals pool pupils' Xmas jumper shame'. TES, 31 May 2019. Available from www.tes.com/news/exclusive-data-reveals-poor-pupils-xmas-jumper-shame [accessed 17 December 2020].

and make it more proactive, as well as increasing your efficiency.

- Understanding the context of your data, and analysing it, allows you to spot emerging safeguarding issues before they become an emergency.
- To be able to use your data well, you need to collect it from a wide range of sources and organise it in the right way.
- Seeing the rich picture allows you to target your resources, work with other agencies, communicate and manage performance internally, and to stand back and see the rich picture.
- The quality of your safeguarding data can have a critical impact on your ability and that of other services to protect victims.

Chapter 8
The challenge of change
Lessons learned

If you've ever found yourself watching a TV news report after a tragic and preventable incident, you'll have seen this kind of scenario.

A be-suited figure stands solemnly at a podium with a microphone, a sheaf of papers laid out before them.

> First of all, I'd like to offer my sincere condolences to the family after this dreadful tragedy. I'd also like to apologise on behalf of my organisation for, on this occasion, falling well below the standards that should be expected of us. And finally, I'd like to reassure people that lessons have been learned from this terrible event so we can prevent anything similar happening again.

Does it sound familiar? Here's a translation: 'I've been on a media training course and have been told to do three things: offer my condolences, apologise, and tell people that "lessons have been learned" so we won't repeat the same mistakes. That way, at least we don't look quite so bad.'

It sounds easy, doesn't it? But in fact, learning lessons (and implementing them) is one of the most difficult things we can ever do. Because the process must take into account not only the variability of human nature, but also the hugely demanding nature of change – especially when it's at a fundamental level. It often requires us to set aside our long-established ways of working and, yes, our prejudices, and embrace new ways of thinking and working. It demands that we challenge our strongly held beliefs and opinions. And it asks that we countenance the need for doing something differently, possibly for the first time. This can seem impossible to perceive, let alone do.

Let's bring this into the personal sphere. We'll start the healthy eating 'tomorrow'. We'll cut down on alcohol 'after Christmas'. We'll be organised about paying our bills on time 'when this month is over'. On a private level, we're familiar with the excuses we give ourselves for maintaining the status quo, even when the benefits of change are staring us in the face. We find ways either to deny the need for it, or to persuade ourselves that it's not that important after all. Our favourite tactic is to say that until some external factor that we have no control over changes, we can't either. *I'll start exercising 'when the weather's better'. I'll save more money 'when I get a pay rise'.* If it's like this for ourselves, why should it be different at an organisational level?

This is why it's always been incredibly difficult to get people to learn, and most importantly, to implement the lessons from safeguarding incidents. What seems a logical imperative that should be carried out instantly can take years or even decades to complete. There's something intransigent in our human reactions to the need for change, and for organisations to transform the way they do things.

A key example is in the sharing of information. This has been permitted by legislation since the Crime and Disorder Act 1988 gave organisations the legal power to share information for the purposes of preventing crime. And yet we still hear debates about whether it's okay for schools to exchange data with external agencies. Despite the fact that the GDPR allows schools to do it, and the Data Protection Act 2018 says they should do it (and gives a framework for carrying it out), practitioners in education, local authorities, the police, healthcare services and other agencies are still debating whether it should happen and if so how to go about it.

And yet, despite how difficult it is to change, it's essential that we do so because the death or serious injury of children and vulnerable adults has been the subject of adverse findings in Serious Case Reviews for too many years. These reviews are now called 'child safeguarding practice reviews' in England (formerly 'Serious Case Reviews'), 'case management reviews' in Northern Ireland, 'significant case reviews' in Scotland, and 'child practice reviews' in Wales. Whatever the name, they involve examining the circumstances leading up to the event to identify who did what, when, and why. They're characterised as opportunities for learning, not for apportioning blame.

If you were to summarise the totality of the lessons that come out of this huge body of evidence, it would be to:

o   pay attention to what's going on;
o   record what's going on, including the small stuff because it paints a bigger picture;
o   share what you know; and
o   take appropriate action.

It really is as simple, and as challenging, as that. The same mistakes that led to tragedies are repeated time and time again, and yet they're not addressed. They demand new training and development programmes; leadership and management attitude shifts; changes in working practices and processes; and the writing of new policies and procedures. What's more, all this must be communicated at every level. It's no picnic, we realise, but even setting aside the *moral* reasons for changing there's a *legal* imperative to do so.

So we know we need to get better at changing, and we know it's difficult. Let's look at *why* we seem to find it so hard.

Why we find it hard to change

People are programmed to be resistant to change, especially if it challenges their established worldview. Also, most organisations are bureaucratic and siloed in their make-up. This is a toxic combination when it comes to making a step change in the way safeguarding is done in your school.

I sympathise, as I had a similar experience while Chief Constable of Dorset Police. Just like you, we had to juggle priorities of varying proportions and were always having to choose which one deserved the most resources. However, when the 2012 Olympics came to the UK I was taught a huge lesson in how change can happen successfully, even if it seems impossible at first.

You may wonder what the Olympics had to do with Dorset, but we were responsible for policing the sailing and windsurfing events. There were 62 nations competing for medals, each with a need for security, and there was always the potential for a terrorist incident or security breach. Also, it was a multi-agency operation, involving local authorities, the police, the fire and rescue service, ambulance, hospitals, the army, navy, air force, private security and the host venue, as well as the National and International Olympic Committees. We had to find new ways of working together, so the need for us to take a radical look at our operations had never been stronger.

However, we had a gift: the fixed date of the event and its stratospherically high profile. Was anyone going to move the Olympics back a few weeks, even if I asked nicely? Of course not. The result was that with the stakes as high as they were, the political will was there to move mountains in a short space of time. Together with our colleagues in those other services, we managed to pull together a well-organised and secure event. It's amazing what a clear political imperative, combined with a set budget and a fixed deadline, can achieve.

This shows that people *can* change their way of working if they really want to, but they have to have a clear and pressing reason to do so. One of the biggest issues with learning safeguarding lessons is that there's rarely that level of clarity or political will (or the resourcing) to make change happen – especially on a macro level.

Resistance to change

It's also worth examining some of the psychological science behind resistance to change, so as to understand it better. Leadership expert David Rock has worked with neuroscientists to develop what he's called his SCARF Model.[1] SCARF stands for the five key 'domains' that influence our social behaviour.

o **Status:** our relative importance to others.
o **Certainty:** our ability to predict the future.
o **Autonomy:** our sense of control over events.
o **Relatedness:** how safe we feel with others.
o **Fairness:** how fair we perceive the exchanges between people to be.

These domains trigger the threat and reward responses in our brains, which interpret them in the same way as our ancestors did for survival. This is why we have such strong emotions about them – we feel like we're in danger if the balance is upset. For instance, suppose you and two other agencies are found to be at fault after a critical incident involving a child at your school. You're asked to make significant changes to the way you work,

[1] Mind Tools, 'David Rock's SCARF Model'. Available from www. mindtools.com/pages/article/SCARF.htm [accessed 17 December 2020].

but the other agencies are not. Logic says you should make the changes anyway for the greater good, but your fairness domain is triggered, which makes you feel threatened and angry. So you drag your heels over the changes or implement them half-heartedly.

This shows that change, if implemented in a way that runs counter to human nature, will never work unless the stakes are enormously high (as they were for the Olympics). However, there's more. Other research has shown that most attempts at change fail not because people make no progress, but because they relapse.[2] If the need for transformation isn't clear and compelling, and if the people responsible for it aren't involved in the change process, and if the changes aren't integrated into everyday work, they're simply harder to sustain. If it doesn't seem urgent and important enough, we slip back into the default way of doing things. That's why it can take years for changes to become the new norm.

We think it's helpful to understand the psychology behind our attitude to change, because when you're thinking about how to implement it in your school you need to take these elements into account. For instance, if you ask one member of staff to alter their processes and they ask why they're the only one, you know you're causing them to focus on the fairness domain.

Getting into the habit of change

So far, we've been talking about significant changes – the kinds of transformations you might want to effect if you've had an incident in your school that wasn't managed well, or have learned something significant that you think would help you do your safeguarding more effectively. Big changes are good when you need them, but more effective is to get into the habit of reviewing

---

[2] B. Steenbarger, 'Why is it so hard to change our behaviour?' *Forbes*, 7 February 2016. Available from www.forbes.com/sites/brettsteenbarger/2016/02/07/why-is-it-so-hard-to-change-our-behavior [accessed 17 December 2020].

your safeguarding practice on a regular basis to prevent problems happening in the first place.

In our experience, and in common with most organisations, schools tend to be incident-driven rather than systematically engaged in routine preventative work. We know how difficult it is to be consistent with this – you're too busy being busy to make the time. But unless you step back from the busyness every now and then and analyse what you're doing, you'll just keep getting even busier. This sounds counter-intuitive, but how much time does it take to sort out a serious problem when it arises, or deal with a major incident that could have been prevented? If you don't take time to reflect, you could just be digging that trench deeper and deeper, only to find out that you're digging in the wrong direction.

Time to reflect – and act

When you think about it, self-reflection is part of your professional life in any case, so why not apply it more widely than just to your teaching? How about, once a quarter, gathering your team to ask yourselves what you've learned in that time? What happened, and what insights came out of it? How could you improve? In safeguarding there's so much you can learn, and the beauty of having a systematic approach is that it makes it easier for you to feed it into a training cycle. That way, your people will be developed to perform at a higher level 'on purpose' rather than it being hit and miss. You'll never reach a point when you don't need to learn any more, because times change and new issues arise every month, so it's best to start from the standpoint that you always have more to discover.

One really good way of learning lessons in 'real time' is to hold regular operational debriefing sessions, which could be a daily or weekly activity with your team (you may already do this). These are a great opportunity for the whole safeguarding team to review workloads, to listen to and learn from others, and to provide practical support and guidance to each other. These are intended to be 'short and sharp' sessions – in our company we call them 'stand ups' and the clue is in the name, because they are not meant to be lengthy, drawn out meetings. These sessions should be supplemented by structured debriefs about particular cases and this is common practice in many organisations (not least the military and the emergency services). These are an opportunity for everyone involved to record what went well (and the reasons why it went well), what didn't go so well (and why) and to agree how to implement the lessons from both success and failure. It could well be appropriate for your MAT CEO, your headteacher or other senior leaders to be involved in structured debriefs and you will want to update them regularly on issues and trends in any event. Sometimes you will want to involve external practitioners (e.g. from partner agencies) in your debriefs and this can be incredibly powerful. Your team and your partners are a fount of knowledge for you to draw on and you should use it; you can't expect or be expected to know everything.

In fact, feeling that we should know everything is one of the reasons we can be resistant to change. That's why it's important for you to create a culture of it being okay to admit mistakes; see each one as a learning opportunity and run some training to ensure that everyone understands what the issue is. Then, when the inspectors arrive and ask you how you learn lessons from your safeguarding practice, you can explain your systematic approach. 'We realised after an incident that we didn't know enough about upskirting, so we found out more about it and included it in our quarterly update training for all staff.' This sounds pretty positive compared to, 'It hasn't happened before and we don't think it will happen again.'

Even better is if you have a central system for recording your learnings. You should be able to record these at any point in the safeguarding process, together with what you've done about them.

This gives you a personal record of professional development. Without a place to put things, it's easy for learnings to dissipate in the wind of daily life.

Learning lessons

So you know that implementing regular learning reviews is a good idea, but what kinds of lessons should they focus on? The best place to start is to go back to your strategic assessment of the issues that face your school. What are the hot topics, and how have you responded to them? Have you done a good job, or not? Next, look at the areas for improvement that you've identified internally but also think about what you've learned from external sources. What's going on out there that you could make use of? Finally, feed all this into your safeguarding improvement plan, which ultimately achieves your objective of preventing harm. It's not complicated when you think about it like this, but you do need to be systematic about it.

Speaking for ourselves, we know it takes personal discipline to be consistent about reflection and learning. We have to make ourselves do it, and have instituted processes to help us. In the same way, you should adopt a mindset of seeing safeguarding as a planned, learning-based activity. If you teach yourself as you go along you'll become consistently better at it – it's impossible not to. In time, you'll find yourself upstream of the learnings, because you'll become more and more aware of what you don't yet know.

Systems thinking

It's one thing setting up processes for learning and change within your safeguarding team (if you have one), but it's another to do it across your school or even more widely than that. This is because systems are notoriously inflexible and don't adapt to the needs of the individuals working in them. People try to make imperfect systems work by driving change locally and hoping it will expand outwards and upwards, but this rarely happens.

And yet you have to think of your school, college or MAT as a whole system, not just as a collection of individuals. It's hard but necessary, as excelling at safeguarding should never be done wholly by one person or even a small group. This relates to something called 'systems thinking', which is a holistic approach to analysing a problem that focuses on the way an organisation's constituent parts interrelate, and how they work in the context of the overall system. The idea is that system behaviour comes from what happens when various parts of the system are reinforced and balanced.[3]

As an example, one of the greatest lessons we had to learn in policing was the need to challenge its historical silo mentality. When the force was first created it was purely about bobbies on the beat; then detectives were added, followed by traffic police, community police, and forensics. There were sound reasons for the evolution of these functions, but when Dorset Police was tasked with removing £10 million from the annual operating budget, we were forced to think about the organisation as one entity. So we adopted a systems thinking approach and asked ourselves: 'What do we need to deliver for the public? Greater safety and less crime. So how can we work holistically to achieve that?'

We then went about organising ourselves to meet those objectives. If a crime was reported, instead of sending uniformed officers as a first response followed later by detectives, we realised it was sometimes more efficient for detectives to attend from the start. And if an incident happened in one neighbourhood but there were no police officers immediately available to respond, we'd

---

[3] Search CIO, 'Definition: systems thinking'. Available from https://searchcio.techtarget.com/definition/systems-thinking [accessed 17 December 2020].

send some from a nearby area, realising that the lines we'd drawn on our maps to divide patrol areas meant nothing to the public. It was the obvious solution, but somehow we'd managed to put our own needs above those of getting the job done. Slowly the divisive walls came tumbling down, breaking up those historical boundaries. This might seem blindingly obvious to you, but when you're working within a system it's difficult to step back and view it in the round.

Implementing 'lessons learned'

When you start to think in a systemic way, one of the most startling revelations is how few of the lessons to be learned are either novel or difficult; it's the implementation that's usually the primary cause of failure. When something goes wrong it tends to be analysed in excruciating detail; you only have to read the findings of public inquiries following awful tragedies to see this. But we rarely ask ourselves *why* things have gone right. Part of learning lessons is picking out the good stuff, recording it, doing more of it, and reinforcing it. This should be the case across the system, because if the outcome of someone taking the initiative and using their professional curiosity was that a child was protected from harm, it's important that everyone relevant knows. If we spent as much time doing this as investigating mistakes, safeguarding would be greatly improved across the board.

We've talked about creating a culture of it being okay to make mistakes (so long as they're not careless ones), but we'd go one step further and suggest that you should go looking for the *near misses*. This is because errors, especially significant ones, tend to be irregular and infrequent; of course you can learn from them, but if you wait for them to happen not only do you increase your risk of a major incident but you'll also not develop as a safeguarding lead. It can be interesting to ask yourself what you've 'got away with' that didn't turn into a tragedy.

Again, we can go back to my time as a Chief Constable to illustrate this. Every morning when I came into work, I'd receive a log of the serious incidents from overnight. It was clear to me when an alert member of staff had caught the ball before it hit the ground and a crisis had been averted, but I was uncomfortably aware that this was sometimes down to our good fortune in having brilliant officers and staff rather than our organisational good judgement. And where were the most experienced and highly paid leaders when these critical decisions were being made in the wee small hours? Tucked up in bed, leaving relatively junior people to take what were often big choices. When I reflected on it, I realised that the reason this way of working was so common in policing nationally was because it harked back to the time when pubs closed early, not many people had cars, and the internet wasn't even dreamed of. So we changed the system by putting some of our more senior people back into their boots at night. It wasn't universally popular by any means, but this proactive measure made the system more robust, as well as providing better leadership and support for our frontline staff.

Learning from data

Thinking more widely than just schools for a moment, there are some major gaps right across the learning system. For instance, in 2019–20 there were 642,980 referrals relating to children in need to social care by police, schools, and other organisations. What can we learn from this? At the macro level, we know how many referrals were made and by whom, and what types of issues they related to. But do we know how many of them were accepted by social care, and how many were rejected and sent back to the originating agency to deal with? Almost certainly not. More importantly, what led to those children becoming 'in need'? In 2019 The Department for Education asked us to contribute to its research to understand which interventions might be most effective for children in need. It was an excellent piece of work but we were left wondering whether this research has filtered down to the operational level where it can be used to make a real difference?[4] Where's the evidence that it has? The government's response to the research was very supportive but short on specifics.[5]

The fact is that governments, local authorities, and other public bodies have more than enough data between them to use techniques such as machine learning to analyse, predict, and prevent many of the harms that affect children and young people. What is needed is the will and the means. If private corporations such as Amazon, Google, and Facebook can predict what we're likely to buy or watch online, it can't be beyond the capabilities of governments to use the data at its disposal in this way.

Sadly, learning and change are hardly ever system-driven, even though they should be. You and your organisation might be able to change something, but your ability to affect the ecosystem in which it operates requires you to develop high levels of trust and co-operation with other agencies. And although many schools, colleges and MATs are starting to challenge the status quo, the debate is still powered by what's going on in public discourse. You only have to look at the number of years it takes for public inquiries to come to a closure to see that, as the proverb says, 'the wheels of change grind exceeding slow and exceeding small'. In fact, they grind the goodness out of the seeds, leaving only empty husks. It's incumbent on the government, policy makers, leaders, and communities to make sure that doesn't happen with safeguarding.

[4] Department for Education, *Help, Protection, Education: Concluding the Children in Need Review*, June 2019. Available from https://assets.publishing. service.gov.uk/government/uploads/system/uploads/attachment_data/ file/809236/190614_CHILDREN_IN_NEED_PUBLICATION_FINAL. pdf [accessed 3 January 2021].

[5] Department for Education, 'Review of children in need' ('Action we will take' section). Available from www.gov.uk/government/publications/ review-of-children-in-need/review-of-children-in-need#action-we-will-take [accessed 17 December 2020].

Key learning points

- Effective learning is an essential pre-requisite for transforming safeguarding practice.
- Learning, and implementing learning, requires strong leadership.
- Learning is at the heart of reducing risk and not repeating mistakes, particularly those that could have tragic consequences.
- It is rare that we don't know what we need to change; the key barrier to change is the failure to systematically implement the available learning.
- Effecting change in response to learning can be hard, both for individuals and institutions, particularly where it challenges cultures, power structures, political timetables, or 'accepted truths'.
- As humans we have a propensity to seek 'silver bullet' solutions; it's far more 'exciting' than having to implement demanding, longer-term programmes of change.
- Systems can support learning by revealing lessons that might not otherwise be visible.
- Learning needs to be regular, proactive, and systematic if it is to be effective; in safeguarding that learning has to be across all agencies.

The future vision

To treat safeguarding as a strategic activity, you need to take a sizeable step back from your day-to-day work and see it in the round. But what does this involve?

1. It means positioning yourself in the hierarchy of your organisation and understanding the roles and responsibilities of governors, trustees, your MAT (if you're in one), head teachers, other leaders, and staff. When you see where you fit in and work out how best to interact with these people, you'll unearth a support structure you might not have known existed.

2. It entails acknowledging that prevention is the core objective of safeguarding. When you have a proactive and systematic approach to spotting signs of harm, you can stop bad things happening and nip problems in the bud. This is surely what we all want to achieve.

3. When you or your staff have a concern or are working with a child who's been harmed, you'll appreciate the importance of managing their case in a holistic way. From taking an initial disclosure, to recording the right information, and working out how to gather the evidence and manage competing priorities within your school, you'll become increasingly expert in this important area.

4. It means feeling confident about working with external agencies. They're there to help you (and vice versa), but it's only when you know how to speak their language and put the relationships to effective use that you'll achieve the joined-up system that the safeguarding community has been seeking for decades.

5. It involves seeing data as your friend. Sharing the right information in the right way is a cornerstone of sound safeguarding, but poor execution in this area has been one of the most intransigent problems to have dogged it for years. When you understand what the law allows you to do and have an open attitude to sharing, you'll be more confident and effective in your role.

6. It means seeing training and developing both for yourself and your staff as one of the keys to enabling safeguarding to thrive in your setting. Gone will be the old-fashioned information-giving sessions and lack of delegation. Instead, you'll be engaging people using scenario-based experiences and involving them in a more productive way. You'll also be clear about the performance and accountabilities of yourself and others, and alive to any dangers within your own organisation.

7. It entails making dynamic use of your safeguarding data. You'll find yourself spotting problems before they become critical, and thinking about how you record information and use it in a fresh light. This allows you to be focused and proactive.

8. Finally, it means seeing improvement as a never-ending process, which isn't necessarily easy but is part of creating a culture of excellence. If you're systematic about it and – even better – if you are able to share your learnings with other organisations, you're well on the way to transforming safeguarding in your setting.

Where should you start? Do you need to tackle every area? And what actions can you take that will give you the best results in the least amount of time? You can't do everything at once, so please don't feel as if you're frozen in the headlights, daunted by the scale of the task ahead.

Your first task is to gain an understanding of where you're currently at in your school. Next, think about the main safeguarding issues to address and consider them in the context of your particular setting and the support you need from governance, leadership, and management. Then, in order to avert harm and to prevent the safeguarding problems you've identified escalating, how should you best respond? Are your current methods for reporting and case managing concerns fit for purpose? And what do you need to do to work more effectively with other agencies, your own staff, or both? If you didn't download and fill in our strategic assessment tool at the beginning of the book, now's a good time to take a look. You can find it at: https://safeguarding. thesafeguardingcompany.com/assessment-tool.

It's worth bearing in mind that it's not usually the case in safeguarding that practitioners don't know (or can't find out) what to do; the issue is that they don't always do it, or systematically keep doing it. It's inevitably more exciting to tackle a new initiative than to focus on what will give you the best result. That's why we advocate not only doing the right things, but doing them regularly and reliably using sound strategic principles. (But that doesn't mean you shouldn't innovate and try out new ideas.)

The future of safeguarding in education

Let's indulge ourselves for a moment. What would the world of safeguarding look like if every organisation with a safeguarding responsibility were to follow the eight principles in this book? It goes without saying that our hope is that children and other vulnerable people would be safer. But there's more than that. Safeguarding leads would feel more confident and in control, and safeguarding in education would be a recognised profession in its own right.

This is our vision too. We'd love to see national standards for the training of safeguarding leads (which may understandably be different in England, Scotland, Wales, and Northern Ireland, although with shared principles); also a code of practice which is regulated. A professional body for safeguarding leads is essential, bringing support and recognition to your vital role. Overall, we want to see the role of the safeguarding lead being professionalised, driving up standards by raising expectations and delivering excellent support and training. At the moment, there's no coherent safeguarding 'industry', and no ongoing, substantial debate or body of knowledge in one place, and there ought to be.

To this end, we've set up our own Safeguarding Advisory Panel with independent external experts, and with them we're starting to create a movement for change. If you'd like to keep in touch with the work we're doing, or to contribute your ideas, please register your interest here: https://safeguarding.thesafeguardingcompany.com/join-in.

It's the least that you deserve, and we're on the case. But in the meanwhile, let's see safeguarding as the profession it ought to be and create a culture of excellence around it. How else will we be able to prove that lessons have been learned?

Afterword

In early 2020, following our completion of the first draft of this book, the global Covid-19 pandemic burst onto the scene. On 18 March, the UK government announced the closure of all nurseries, schools, and colleges in England 'until further notice', other than for the children of key workers and others who were vulnerable or in particular need. This was on the back of previously announced school closures in Wales, Scotland, and Northern Ireland. As we go to press in March 2021 schools and colleges across the UK are just emerging from the third such lockdown.

We've already detailed the enormous and ever-increasing challenges and complexities in education safeguarding. We can now add to this the risks created by the pandemic: the social, cultural, and financial impact of the disease; the differential effect of the disease on the health of black and minority ethnic communities; the fallout for the low paid, the unemployed, and families already living in poverty; and the frightening challenges encountered by those managing the virus. At the time of writing (March 2021), we are just starting to recover from the latest wave of the pandemic and it has just been reported that the number of recorded incidents of children dying or being seriously harmed after suspected abuse or neglect rose by 27% after England's first lockdown last year.[1] There is no doubt that we are living in the most challenging and demanding period for safeguarding in our lifetimes. When we consider the current overstretch of *all* public services, it's easy to see that the burden on safeguarding leads in education is in danger of becoming intolerable.[2]

In closing, we want to say directly to safeguarding leads that you have our unbounded admiration for your incredible dedication, resilience, and commitment to the wellbeing of children. 'Above and beyond' is what you were doing prior to the pandemic; there are no words sufficient to thank you or to praise you highly enough for the personal sacrifices you have made and continue to make during this pandemic to support families and to protect children from harm. If anyone ever deserved a round of applause (and, of far greater utility, much more support) it's you. We're with you for the long run.

---

[1] The Child Safeguarding Practice Review Panel received 285 serious incident notifications from April to September 2020. This is an increase of 27% from 225 in the same period in 2019. Gov.uk, 'Part 1 (April to September) 2020-21: Serious incident notifications', 15 January 2021. Available from https://explore-education-statistics.service.gov.uk/find-statistics/serious-incident-notifications; BBC News, 'Covid-19: Rise in suspected child abuse cases after lockdown', 17 January 2021. Available from www.bbc.co.uk/news/uk-55682745 [accessed 17 January 2021].

[2] During the course of the first pandemic lockdown in the spring of 2020, we introduced regular safeguarding support webinars that were open to any safeguarding lead wanting to attend. Over the course of the following six months, we worked with several thousand education safeguarding leads from across the UK and around the world. We also worked with Professor Jonathan Crego from the Hydra Foundation who conducted an academically rigorous online debrief of 250 safeguarding leads to record their lived experience of safeguarding during the pandemic and in the course of this book we have addressed many of the issues they raised. The full debrief report can be found at https://safeguarding.thesafeguardingcompany.com/blog/safeguarding-in-education-during-covid-lessons-learned/.

Appendix

Each of the four UK nations has its own laws and guidance that set out the safeguarding responsibilities of schools and colleges. Below is a summary of the primary sources of this guidance in England, Wales, Scotland, and Northern Ireland.

England

The safeguarding duties of schools and colleges are set out in section 175 of the Education Act 2002, the Education (Independent School Standards) Regulations 2014, and the Non-Maintained Special Schools (England) Regulations 2015.

Working Together to Safeguard Children (HM Government 2018)
www.gov.uk/government/publications/working-together-to-safeguard-children--2

Keeping Children Safe in Education – For Schools and Colleges (Department for Education 2020)
www.gov.uk/government/publications/keeping-children-safe-in-education--2

Governance Handbook (Department for Education 2020)
www.gov.uk/government/publications/governance-handbook

Competency Framework for Governance (Department for Education 2017)
www.gov.uk/government/publications/governance-handbook

Sexual Violence and Sexual Harassment Between Children in Schools and Colleges (Department for Education 2018)
www.gov.uk/government/publications/sexual-violence-and-sexual-harassment-between-children-in-schools-and-colleges

Guidance for independent schools (Department for Education 2019)
www.gov.uk/government/publications/regulating-independent-schools

Wales

Future Generations Act 2015
https://gov.wales/sites/default/files/publications/2019-08/well-being-of-future-generations-wales-act-2015-the-essentials.pdf

Working Together to Safeguard People (Welsh Government 2019)
https://gov.wales/safeguarding-people-introduction

Wales Safeguarding Procedures (Welsh Government 2019)
https://safeguarding.wales/

Keeping Learners Safe (Welsh Government 2020)
https://gov.wales/keeping-learners-safe

Making a Difference: A Guide for the Designated Person for Looked After Children in Schools (Welsh Government 2017)
https://gov.wales/sites/default/files/publications/2018-11/making-a-difference-a-guide-for-the-designated-person-for-looked-after-children-in-schools.pdf

Scotland

The Children (Scotland) Act 1995 places a duty on schools and local authorities to safeguard and promote the welfare of children.
https://education.gov.scot/education-scotland/who-we-are/policies-and-information/safeguarding

Getting It Right for Every Child (GIRFEC) (Scottish Government)
www.gov.scot/policies/girfec

National Guidance for Child Protection in Scotland (Scottish Government 2014)
www.gov.scot/publications/national-guidance-child-protection-scotland

At the time of writing, the Scottish Government was consulting on a revised version of the National Guidance for Child Protection to ensure its consistency with the legislative and policy framework and current practice developments. It plans to publish online the final revised National Guidance in spring 2021.
www.gov.scot/publications/consultation-revised-national-guidance-child-protection-scotland-2020/

Northern Ireland

Understanding the Needs of Children in Northern Ireland (UNOCINI) Guidance (Department of Health 2011)
www.health-ni.gov.uk/publications/understanding-needs-children-northern-ireland-unocini-guidance

Co-operating to Safeguard Children and Young People in Northern Ireland (Department of Health 2017)
www.health-ni.gov.uk/publications/co-operating-safeguard-children-and-young-people-northern-ireland

Safeguarding and Child Protection in Schools – A Guide for Schools (Department of Education 2019)
www.education-ni.gov.uk/publications/safeguarding-and-child-protection-schools-guide-schools (updated 3 September 2020)

Child Protection Support Service – School Governors Handbook (Department of Education 2019)
www.education-ni.gov.uk/publications/child-protection-support-service-school-governors-handbook

UNOCINI – Understanding the Needs of Children in Northern Ireland – Thresholds of Need Model (Education Authority Northern Ireland 2018)
www.eani.org.uk/sites/default/files/2018-10/UNOCINI%20-%20Thresholds%20of%20Need%20Model.pdf

A timeline of child protection and safeguarding in the UK

While the practice of child abuse goes back to the roots of human history, it is only in the last century or so that it has been recognized as a distinct phenomenon, something that children have a right to be protected from.

Barbara Bilston, the Open University[1]

When you're looking at safeguarding from a strategic perspective, it's helpful to see today's practice in the context of what's gone before. We hope you find this timeline of child protection and safeguarding interesting; it's been constructed from several helpful articles.[2]

---

[1] B. Bilston, 'A history of child protection'. *OpenLearn*, updated 30 August 2019. Available from www.open.edu/openlearn/body-mind/childhood-youth/working-young-people/history-child-protection [accessed 17 December 2020].

[2] D. Batty, 'Timeline: a history of child protection'. *The Guardian*, 18 May 2005. Available from www.theguardian.com/society/2005/may/18/childrensservices2; NSPCC Learning, 'History of child protection in the

1889: The NSPCC was formed and the act known as the 'Children's Charter' was passed. This allowed the law to intervene between parents and children for the first time in history, giving police the power to apply for a warrant to enter a home if a child was thought to be in danger. Five years later, the act was extended to allow children to give evidence in court, and it became an offence to deny a sick child medical treatment.

These protections soon expanded into child welfare: school meals, free milk, and medical care raised the health levels of children.

1908: The Children's Act 1908 established juvenile courts and brought in the registration of foster parents. The Punishment of Incest Act made sexual abuse illegal, rather than just being a matter for the church.

1932: The Children and Young Person's Act was passed. Its main tenet was to set standards for working conditions for young people leaving school, but it also established the principle of supervision of young people when outside the home. As such, it laid the foundation for modern local authority children's services. The following year, all existing child protection legislation was brought into a single law.

1945: Following the death of 12-year-old Dennis O'Neill at the hands of his foster parents, the Parliamentary Care of Children Committee was established. In 1948, the Children Act established the presence of a children's committee and officer in each local authority. The issues that contributed to Dennis's death were identified as 'poor record-keeping and filing, unsuitable appointments, lack of partnership working, resource concerns,

UK'. Available from https://learning.nspcc.org.uk/child-protection-system/history-of-child-protection-in-the-uk/; B. Bilston, 'A history of child protection'. *OpenLearn*, updated 30 August 2019. Available from www.open.edu/openlearn/body-mind/childhood-youth/working-young-people/history-child-protection [all articles accessed 17 December 2020].

failing to act on warning signs, weak supervision and "a lamentable failure of communication"'.[3]

1973: The inquiry into the death of Maria Colwell highlighted a lack of co-ordination between the services responsible for child welfare. This led to the development of Area Child Protection Committees in England and Wales, and the establishment of our modern child protection system.

1989: The Children Act 1989 established the legislative framework for the current child protection system in England and Wales, followed in 1995 by similar frameworks in Scotland and Northern Ireland. It also gave children the right to protection from abuse and exploitation; its central theme was that children are best looked after by their families.

1995: The Children (Scotland) Act incorporated the three key principles of the UN Convention on the Rights of the Child into Scottish law: protection from discrimination, ensuring child welfare is a primary concern, and listening to children's views.

1999: The Protection of Children Act was passed; its aim was to prevent paedophiles from working with children. A similar act was passed in Scotland in 2003.

2003: Lord Laming published his report into the death of Victoria Climbié, which found that numerous opportunities to save her had been missed. A government green paper, *Every Child Matters*, proposed an electronic tracking system for England's children, the creation of children's trusts, a children's director, and a children's commissioner for England.

2004: The Children Act 2004 pushed forward the main proposals of the green paper and was passed by parliament. Although it

---

[3] Community Care, 'What have we learned? Child death scandals since 1944', 10 January 2007. Available from www.communitycare.co.uk/2007/01/10/ what-have-we-learned-child-death-scandals-since-1944/ [accessed 3 January 2021].

allowed local authorities flexibility in some areas, it mandated that each should appoint a children's director and replace ACPCs with Local Safeguarding Children Boards (LSCBs).

2006: The statutory guidance *Working Together to Safeguard Children* was released, outlining multi-agency working.

2008: The death of Peter Connelly led to further reviews of social service care in England. In 2009, Lord Laming's report, *The Protection of Children in England,* made 58 recommendations for child protection reforms.

2011: The Munro report, *A Child-Centred System,* made recommendations that attempted to stop the child protection system from being overly bureaucratic and compliance-orientated, and more about keeping children safe.

2012: Operation Yewtree was set up to investigate sexual abuse allegations against Jimmy Savile.

2013: An independent review was set up into child sexual exploitation in Rochdale, questioning the council's approach to the events in the area. In addition, a Serious Case Review was published in relation to the death of Daniel Pelka, who died from head injuries inflicted by his parents.

2014: The Social Services and Well-being (Wales) Act 2014 gave Wales its own legislative framework for social services. Also, the Children and Well-being Act was given royal assent, bestowing greater protection on vulnerable children.

2015: The Independent Inquiry into Child Sexual Abuse in England and Wales (IICSA) was launched to examine growing evidence of institutional failures to protect children from sexual abuse. In addition, *Keeping Children Safe in Education* was published, giving statutory guidance for schools and colleges on the safeguarding of children and on safer recruitment.

2017: The Digital Economy Act increased protection from online pornography, by allowing sites that display it to children to be blocked in the UK.

2018: *Working Together to Safeguard Children* was updated for England, and replaced LSCBs with local safeguarding partner arrangements.

The authors

Martin Baker QPM

Martin's policing career spanned five UK police forces, including significant spells in counter-terrorism in London and in homicide investigation. As Director of Public Protection for Gwent Police, he was responsible for all aspects of safeguarding and child protection, and as the Assistant Chief Constable for Gloucestershire he managed (among other things) the risks posed by violent and sexual offenders living in the community.

Martin's most recent policing role was as Chief Constable of Dorset Police. During his time there, his officers and staff delivered eight consecutive years of crime reduction while achieving national 'best in class' public satisfaction – the highest levels of public confidence for any police force in England and Wales. His force also won the prestigious Sunday Times top 75 Companies Award, and achieved Investors in People. In 2006, he was awarded The Queen's Medal for Distinguished Police Service (QPM).

Today, Martin is CEO and co-founder of The Safeguarding Company, the makers of MyConcern. He's also an experienced school governor in both primary and upper schools, and is currently a director of a multi-academy trust.

Mike Glanville

Mike had a varied career in the police service, most recently as a chief police officer. As a young detective he was a trained Child Protection Officer, a role which involved managing serious and complex child abuse cases; later, as Head of CID, he was responsible for all child and adult safeguarding cases. He also led on a number of critical incidents and major crime investigations involving vulnerable children and adults, and was the chair of the Local Criminal Justice Board in Dorset, representing the force at the Local Children's Safeguarding Board.

His most recent role was Assistant Chief Constable for Dorset Police, responsible for the delivery of operational policing across the county, including adult and child protection services. Currently he's Chief Safeguarding Officer at The Safeguarding Company, with responsibility for ensuring that the latest best practice is integrated into the range of products and services delivered by the company. He also oversees all aspects of safeguarding training, using his knowledge and understanding of the challenges faced by safeguarding practitioners.

Mike is regularly invited to speak at national and international conferences and events to share his expertise on safeguarding. He too is an experienced school governor, and has been a Chair of Governors for over 10 years.

About MyConcern

One Team Logic is a safeguarding company that provides a full range of safeguarding products and services.

MyConcern is our secure, state-of-the-art online safeguarding recording and case management system. Designed by our team of safeguarding experts, built by our world-class development team, and continually developed to meet the needs of its users, MyConcern is trusted by safeguarding leads across the UK and around the world. In 2018 MyConcern won the Queen's Award for Enterprise in the Innovation category.

Our customers include schools and colleges, local authorities, sports organisations, housing associations, governing bodies, charities, and faith groups. The platform enables users to record safeguarding and wellbeing concerns, and the organisation's safeguarding lead to manage them; this can be done on a multi-agency basis if needed. It ensures that all the information needed to protect individuals, and to manage safeguarding cases, is available in a secure and easy-to-access system. This means that users can spot trends and be proactive in safeguarding the children and young people in their care. MyConcern also enables users to create a wide range of reports in various formats to support timely, well-informed decision-making. You can find more information about MyConcern at www.thesafeguardingcompany.com.

Sentry: alongside MyConcern we provide Sentry, a safeguarding software tool that manages the safer recruitment process in schools, colleges, and a wide range of other organisations. In educational settings Sentry is also the establishment's Single Central Record. Sentry ensures that recruitment processes are robust, and acts as a critical first line of defence against people who may present significant risks to children and young people. You can find more information about Sentry at www. thesafeguardingcompany.com/sentry.

Clarity is MyConcern's multi-establishment reporting platform, which gives organisations access to customisable reports and data exports across a range of establishments or sites (such as across schools in a MAT or local authority area). High-level, anonymised reporting provides insights, identifies trends, and tracks progress, helping to ensure that safeguarding responsibilities are met. Clarity enables schools to pinpoint where specific issues are occurring so they can allocate resources appropriately. They can also create reports over time to show the impact of interventions. You can find more information about Clarity at www. thesafeguardingcompany.com/clarity.

Safeguarding services: we offer a range of high-quality CPD-certified training courses for safeguarding leads, governors, trustees, board members, and frontline staff in education and in other settings, as well as a range of other professional services. You can find more information at www.thesafeguardingcompany. com/mentor.

Free resources: to get access to our extensive range of free safeguarding resources, just visit our Resource Hub at www. thesafeguardingcompany.com/resource-hub.

Acknowledgements

During our policing careers we encountered countless people who became victims or perpetrators (and sometimes both) purely as a result of their own adverse childhood experiences; the names, faces, and stories of many will be with us forever and their tragic stories still motivate us daily. When we retired from policing, we both felt there was 'unfinished business' and that we had another contribution to make. It was almost by chance we discovered what that contribution was to be and it remains a work in progress.

In all our involvement with schools and colleges, we've had the great good fortune to be inspired by many people, mostly safeguarding leads but also many other teaching and non-teaching members of school and college staff. We owe a particular debt of gratitude to Helen Williams, Angela Maxted, Jackie Shanks, Lisa Atack, Catherine Smith, Adam Lubbock, Caroline Newman, Luke Ramsden, and Sue Bailey MBE, from whom we have learned so much. Their leadership, drive, and determination to improve safeguarding are like rocket fuel for the soul. We say to them: you're the torch bearers for your colleagues everywhere.

We also want to thank our co-founder at The Safeguarding Company, Darryl Morton, and our amazing team, whose commitment to safeguarding is truly awe-inspiring.

Finally, we must thank Ginny Carter who used her incredible organisational and editing talents to help us make this book a reality, and the many friends, colleagues, and safeguarding leads who read early drafts and told us what they *really* thought. Feedback is a gift!

Index

Lightning Source UK Ltd.
Milton Keynes UK
UKHW021821191022
410751UK00014B/2083